HOW TO GET FIRED AT THE C-LEVEL

HOW TO GET **FIRED** AT THE C-LEVEL

Why mismanaging change
is the biggest risk of all

Peter Taylor

First published in 2017 by
The Lazy Project Manager Ltd
3 Foxwood Drive
Binley Woods
Coventry
CV3 2SP

A CIP catalogue record for this book is available from the British Library

ISBN 978–0–9576689–7–3

I would like to dedicate this book to the real custodians of change – from the executive leaders who truly understand change (and therefore projects) – to the project sponsors who take ownership and direct that change, and to the thousands of professional project managers who deliver amazing results every day that bring about positive change.

Contents

Acknowledgements

I would like to thank all those who contributed to this book and to the many years of project experience that has led to this point in time.

Change has been a major part of my life, as it is for everyone of course, but change through projects and project management has been my motivation and driver for many years.

Personal change has led to the creation of my alter-ego 'The Lazy Project Manager' under which guise I thank all of those organisations that have engaged me to speak at their business events, something I am always delighted to do, as well as the many thousands of people who are connected to me on LinkedIn, follow me on Twitter (@thelazypm), listen to my podcasts in iTunes (The Lazy Project Manager) and read my – hopefully – humorous, challenging and occasionally irreverent (but always with a desire to make life better) blogs.

Professional change has placed me in a position of senior leadership for a very large community of 'agents of change', professionals overseeing thousands of projects for many hundreds of customers with millions of users, all of whom are led by C-level executives who are driving strategic change within their own organisations, and no doubt aiming to do that successfully.

I hope this book helps a little.

Thank you, *Peter*

Foreword

Ian Campbell

Ex CEO Airtel-Vodafone and CEO for Airfi

To survive in today's fast-changing world and compete in a technologically driven global economy businesses are having to adapt quickly. Agility, scalability and the ability to engage with the new, smart globalized Millennials who prefer contract working to the stifling office environment are key to playing the game. It has never been truer that 'knowledge is king'. Controlling projects in this new, complex environment has become more complex, yet there is the opportunity for smart businesses to use modern tools, techniques and the new Millennial workforce to achieve their goals in a more agile, cost-efficient manner.

Peter Taylor is quite right in his prognosis that, increasingly, C-level executives need to consider their ability to manage their resources in this new, complex world.

Peter highlights the point that among 1,000 board members from 286 public and private organisations that were fired, or otherwise forced out, the number one reason for their untimely departure was 'mismanaging change!'

If you are a C-level executive, I therefore urge you to invest time to read this fascinating book.

Airfi (www.airfinetworks.com)

The Internet of Things is predicted to become the largest device market in the world and in the next few years will grow to double the size of the smartphone, PC, tablet, connected car and wearables markets combined.

Airfi was created to help equipment manufacturers adopt cellular connectivity in the products they build, ensuring that the complexities of how these networks operate are simplified.

Alex Marson, MD Tailwind PS

Co-Founder & Director at Tailwind Project Solutions

I have known Peter Taylor for more than twelve years. In that time he has transitioned from Cognos to Siemens then Infor is now Global Head of the PMO at Kronos. I remember when he published his first book The Lazy Project Manager and kicked off his speaking career, and how engaging and natural he was. He challenges the norm and seems to be quite comfortable in almost pushing the controversial approach.

This is certainly the case in what is now his eighteenth book - which highlights how critical it is for those at C-level to sit up and recognise that their businesses thrive on change, which comes about through the successful delivering of projects. No longer can we accept that projects are handed down the rung of the ladder to employees as an add-on to their current position. In order to survive, C-levels need to get to grips with the strategic importance that change represents to their organisations!

I would highly recommend this book sits on the desk of every CEO/CFO/CIO, and not just sits there but is opened, read and regularly referenced.

Tailwind PS (www.tailwindps.com)

Tailwind Project Solutions was formed to provide a bespoke approach to project leadership development. The organisation works with large FTSE 250 clients including some of the biggest companies in the world in the Asset Management, Professional Services, Software, Automotive, Finance and Pharmaceutical industry, utilising a team of world-class experts to provide a bespoke approach to the challenges that our clients have.

The company was formed as a result of a gap in the market for expertise which truly gets to the heart of the issues clients are facing – providing a robust, expert solution to change the way that companies run their projects.

"Progress is impossible without change, and those who cannot change their minds cannot change anything."

George Bernard Shaw

Introduction

A four-year study by LeadershipIQ.com[1], which interviewed more than 1,000 board members from 286 public and private organisations that fired, or otherwise forced out, their chief executive found that the number one reason CEO's got fired was ... wait for it ... mismanaging change!

Does that surprise you in any way?

Does that worry you in any way?

Research for this book identified a similar pattern of failure through the lack of understanding of the 'project world' by C-level executives[2] and an associated strategic and organisational change management failure as a result of ignorance and a passivity of control for these critical investments.

And so the cry goes up: 'Executives – stop failing your projects!'

Yes, you read that right – not 'stop your failing projects' but 'stop failing your projects'.

In the past you might well have read and heard a lot about the latter, the need to bring a halt to the failure of projects, and that remains true even today, even after the significant investments that have been made in the world of project management and project managers. But I personally, and strongly, believe that the challenge right now is not at the project level but at the executive level.

Hence, 'Executives – stop failing your projects!'

The report 'Why good strategies fail: Lessons for the C-suite' published by the Economist Intelligence Unit Limited[3] concluded that there was a need for increased C-suite attention to change (and therefore projects) 'Leadership support is the most important factor in successful strategy execution, yet a substantial number of survey respondents indicate that the C-suite is insufficiently involved.'

On the subject of finding the right level of C-suite engagement the report declares:

> ... one of the most worrying findings of our survey is that leading executives at a large number of companies do too little about strategy implementation. Only 50% of respondents say that strategy implementation secures the appropriate C-suite attention at their organisation. Similarly, 28% admit that individual projects or initiatives to put strategy into place do not typically receive the necessary senior-level sponsorship.

This book will explore this challenge, and since all challenges are also opportunities, will not only show ways to significantly reduce project failures but also demonstrate how to significantly raise the capability, speed, and success rates of delivering strategic change.

Strategy is change, and change is delivered by projects, but we are naturally averse to change. Yet ignoring ownership of strategic change can, as we have already seen, be an extremely risky path for any executive.

That is why How to get fired at the C-level makes the loud and bold challenge that executives are failing their projects. By direct association, they are therefore failing their businesses by putting the many millions of investment money at risk through ignorance, lack of care, and downright poor professionalism. This situation needs to stop – now!

But this book also offers a simple means to evaluate executive engagement, and to offer a series of very practical steps to let you be the person who puts the 'C' for change into the C-level.

1. It's a commonly held belief that the CEO gets fired (or forced to resign or retire under pressure) because of 'current financial performance'. But that's wrong, according to a study by LeadershipIQ.com. It found that 31% of get fired for poor change management, 28% for ignoring customers, 27% for tolerating low performers, 23% for denying reality and 22% for too much talk and not enough action. The four-year study by LeadershipIQ.com, the world leader in online leadership training, uncovered these results after interviewing 1,087 board members from 286 public, private, business and healthcare organizations that fired, or otherwise forced out, their chief executive.

2 C-level is an adjective used to describe high-ranking executive titles within an organisation. C, in this context, stands for 'Chief'. Officers who hold C-level positions are typically considered the most powerful and influential members of an organisation.

3. *Why good strategies fail: Lessons for the C-suite* published by The Economist Intelligence Unit Limited in 2013

There is nothing permanent except change.

Heraclitus

1

How to get fired at the C-level

We can start easily enough with a look at how to stop. Stop being a C-level executive, or at least stop being one in your current organisation.

This really isn't the purpose of this book but for balance it is important to include a simple guide on how to achieve this, if it really is what you want to achieve of course. It is, after all the title of the book so we would be remiss in not covering this at the very beginning.

Through the eyes of organisations around the world, a survey commissioned specifically for this book, and through thoughts from executives and project leaders, we can see the simple path to getting fired at the C-level.

1.1 The easy way

Just carry on doing what you are doing and eventually you might be included in a corporate announcement that includes one of the following dreaded lines, [your name here] has decided to move on:

- due to health issues;
- to spend more time with their family;
- to pursue other career opportunities.

Or perhaps it will be veiled in an apparent promotion; we are delighted to announce that [your name here] has been moved to the board (and, unspoken in the announcement, is soon to be silently removed).

Obviously this makes for an extremely short book but if you are reading this to find out how to actually get fired at the C-level then there are other ways of course.

In a global survey of 500 removals of CEOs/CFOs over the last 10 years in a selection of Fortune 500, FTSE 500 and Europe 500 companies it was found that methods of removal included:

Death – 3% found the ultimate way out through death in service, probably not much of a career move, definitely not a positive life move, and certainly not recommended as the best escape from the pressure of C-level management. Health was also cited in 2% of cases.

Personal issues – these caused 4% to move on. In some cases, this may well be true of course but they are probably the minority of cases.

Other opportunities – 8% made the voluntary (as we are led to believe) break to move on to new, and presumably better, opportunities.

Scandal – 7% did something that really upset their peers, from affairs to corruption, and this ensured a swift departure.

There are happy endings in the C-level world of course, with 36% of those covered in the survey heading off to retirement and, presumably, a chance to enjoy the fruits of their many years of labour. But a closer inspection reveals that in quite a few cases retirement came about due to:

- Health issues;
- The desire to spend more time with their family;
- Personal issues;
- Hints of scandal;
- Political infighting (and loss in the retiring C-level executive's case).

Perhaps the perfect formula, avoiding the whole 'death in service' option for now – we can leave that as a fallback option or plan B, I guess – is to undertake some wild scandal involving both the company's money and another C-level executive's wife or husband (delete as appropriate), whilst pursuing an opportunity with a rival organisation. This could easily lead you to experience a major health issue. No wonder you have no time to attend to the major strategic objectives with which you have tasked the organisation. That should do it!

It's certainly a tough world out there, and for those at the top of the organisational tree it can really be challenging, which is why it makes no sense to ignore what can be the number one reason for failure – mismanaging the process of strategic change through project-based activity.

Yes, you have plenty of other matters to take care of but change needs to be accorded its due importance.

1.2 The just as easy way

By all means keep up the affairs and the corporate skulduggery but as a source of extra inspiration, it may interest you to know that as part of the research for this book, a survey was undertaken looking at executive change leadership[4].

This research identified a certain pattern of failure, notably through lack of understanding of the project world by C-level executives, and through an associated strategic and organisational change-management failure which came about as a result of both ignorance of and/ or a passivity of control regarding these critical investments.

For in depth analysis of the survey please take a look at the appendices. The high level points from the research were:

Visibility of the full project portfolio is often non-existent – only the 'top' change initiatives were reported at the C-level. Much of the rest of the investment in change was managed and reported at a lower level only, and yet still offered risk of failure.

With an average portfolio value declared of $40m the 'true' value of investment is often underestimated, and therefore focus and leadership was often absent or misdirected.

The strategic change investments did not always deliver progressive change, despite belief at the C-level that this was the case.

Faith in underlying change-delivery capability was very low: less than 20% of respondents felt they could state unreservedly that such capability was consistently good.

---

4   The survey was conducted during May and June 2016 and received responses from organisations around the world ranging from under 100 employees to over 10,000 employees with a breadth of reported number of projects undertaken on an annual basis from less than 10 to over 100 at cost of up to $100m.

The custodians of executive change, the sponsors, were very often unskilled and unprepared to lead such demanding change activities, and relied in many cases on lower level management to fill the gap.

Time, as with many things, was an issue – only 15% of C-level executives were felt to invest an appropriate amount of time in overseeing the changes that they initiated – too many stopped caring after the business case was approved it seems.

Put all the above together and what you have, I would strongly argue, is a potentially weak foundation for successful delivery of significant change within an organisation.

This naturally leads to higher risk of failure.

Or to put that another way – the opportunity to mismanage change is very high.

And that, as we know, is one clear way to get fired at the C-level.

So there you have it – how to get fired at the C-level – simple.

But I am pretty sure this isn't where you would want to leave the subject and so we will move on to the counter, and more positive, consideration of how *not* to get fired at the C-level.

What should you be considering and what should you be doing to make sure your change, your projects, your organisation and, of course, you are still around for the foreseeable future?

It goes back to the two questions I asked at the start of this chapter: 'Did that surprise you in any way?' and 'Does that worry you in any way?'

Change is the law of life. And those who look only to the past or present are certain to miss the future.

John F. Kennedy

2

How not to get fired at the C-level

Having explored this challenge, and seen some simple ways to not be a C-level executive any more, we will turn our attention to how to avoid these mistakes and not only 'not' get fired but explore how to benefit from the world of strategic change, both personally and for your organisation.

Remember, since all challenges are also opportunities, we will show ways to not only significantly reduce project failures but also significantly raise the capability, speed, and success rates of delivering strategic change.

Strategy is change, change is delivered by projects, but we are naturally averse to change, from which comes the first problem or challenge. Ignoring ownership of strategic change can, as we have seen, be an extremely risky path for any executive, so there is the second problem or challenge.

2.1 Why it is now time to alter the way that C-level executives drive change

OK so obviously the idea isn't to help you get fired. As we have seen that is pretty easy to do and you probably don't need a book to tell you how to bring about that result. Instead we want to help you stay put and succeed, particularly when it comes to overseeing significant change within your organisation.

What we really want to talk about now is what you should be considering and what should you be doing to make sure your change, your projects, you and the business that you represent don't disappear into the great conference room in the sky, but instead stay right where they should be, and deliver value.

Therefore, we will begin by exploring why it is now time to alter the way that C-level executives drive change within their organisations before looking at the impact such change can have with a simple lesson in understanding the true value and cost of change within a business.

Change is inevitable, except from a vending machine, it is often joked, and change, to drive strategic initiatives from the boardroom down, is also essential. So let's explore this world of change and see what C-level executives should be doing to make this change happen with the best possible outcome.

2.2 Why change is challenging (and often resisted)

It might well be that you, or some in your organisation, don't understand why change, strategic change, isn't 'just happening'. After all you have reviewed and approved numerous business cases, sanctioned programmes and projects, released funds … yet change is still not happening the way you, the board, or your peers expected it to happen.

Here it might be worthwhile considering some of the basic dynamics of change. Every project that takes place within your organisation is a change: small, medium, large or truly world-shaking – they are all changes.

And people don't like change.

You don't like change. I don't like change. But we live in a world of change.

Without reaching some sort of 'escape velocity' (as in space flight) you will never do anything different. Deciding to be different or to bring about some form of change is most often easiest done when you have no choice in the matter, when outside forces give you no option other than to change. But we are talking here about reaching the point of conscious decision to make a change. In the business world change comes about through a desire to direct the organisation in a certain way, to achieve new growth, to tackle new markets, release new products, expand horizons, comply with regulations and much more.

Any organisational change impacts people – groups and individuals – and this is where it gets complicated.

People on the whole don't like change. But we live in a world of change that is created around us by strategic business objectives.

Look at it this way.

The change dynamic can be described as **C**(urrent), that is where you are now, **D**(esire), where you want to be and **B**(enefit), which is the resultant reward for whatever change is undertaken. An **E**(ffect) can force a change.

For example

E(ffect): My house feels crowded and noisy, and on top of that I have nowhere to put things. This is making life less pleasant!

The needed change dynamic can be described as: My current house is too small (C), I would like a bigger house (D), the benefit of having a bigger house would be more room for myself and my family (B).

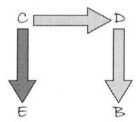

E(ffects) are also important because they will force a change

Figure 1 The change dynamic

Now you may be in any of a number of states as far as change is concerned:

- You may lack any insight to the problem or the need for change to help you bring about some form of life change.

- You may have insight but need a solution or plan.

- You may have insight and a plan but need some assistance in making it happen.

For example:

- Lack of insight – Why does my house seem so crowded and noisy, with nowhere to put things?

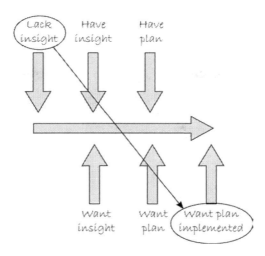

Figure 2 The states of change

- Insight but no plan – My house is too small what shall I do?

- Insight and plan – My house is too small, I need to move, how will I do this?

Warning: we are about to head off into science again.

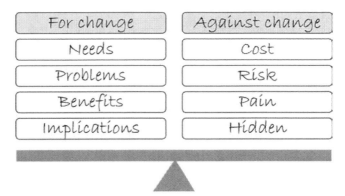

Figure 3 The balance of change

Against change

To move anyone towards change there is a balancing act that needs to be performed. There are a number of resistances that stop change taking place, or at least allow you to put up personal arguments against changing (these might be those small voices in your head that you hear from time to time):

- Cost – Everything has a perceived cost whether this is actual money that would need to be invested or just your time and effort (and distraction from other matters).

- Risk – A concern over what such change would bring about should it in some way fail and require recovery, the work to be redone or loss of face. Concern about the risk of failure and what that would mean to you and others.

- Pain – Recognition that change usually means some form of pain that needs to be endured, the negative aspects of the process of change itself.

- Hidden – It is often possible to uncover the first three points but there will often remain 'hidden' reasons that someone is resistant to such change. If this is you then it is a matter of being honest with yourself, if you are looking to assess the desire for change in others then this is harder to understand.

This makes it hard to assess the 'balance' of resistance since while it may be possible to quantify and address the 'cost', 'risk' and 'pain' elements the 'hidden' ones remain hidden and therefore unquantifiable.

For change

On the other side of the balancing scales are the reasons for change:

- Needs – The definable drivers for adopting a process of change, the need of the person to make a change.

- Problems – What is it that is causing some issue or concern in the status quo that offers the desire to make some form of change?

- Benefits – What are the desirable benefits of such change, the expected beneficial outcomes of adopting something new?

- Implications – If no change is initiated then what will the impact be, what will the consequences be? The implication being that something must be encouraging the need for change in the first place.

Therefore, you need to make sure that the scales fall more heavily on the side of 'for change' in order to stand a chance of making such change a reality. Fail to make that happen and you have no realistic chance of realising change.

Formula for Change

The Formula for Change was created by Richard Beckhard and David Gleicher, refined by Kathie Dannemiller and is sometimes called Gleicher's Formula[5].

This formula (D x V x F x CL > R) provides a model for assessing the relative strengths affecting the likely success or otherwise of organisational change programmes.

Three factors must be present for meaningful organisational change to take place. These factors are:

- D = Dissatisfaction with how things are now

---

5   The original formula, as created by Gleicher and authored by Beckhard and Harris, is: C = (ABD) > X where C is change, A is the status quo dissatisfaction, B is a desired clear state, D is practical steps to the desired state, and X is the cost of the change. It was Kathleen Dannemiller who dusted off the formula and simplified it, making it more accessible for consultants and managers.

- V = Vision of what is possible

- F = First, concrete steps that can be taken towards the vision

- CL = Creative Leadership to navigate towards the vision

If the product of these four factors is greater than

- R = Resistance

then change is possible. Because D, V, and F are multiplied, if any one of them is absent or low, then the product will be low or zero and therefore not capable of overcoming the resistance.

2.3 How can the C-level better deliver change?

First of all C-level executives need to understand that strategic change, at the executive level, is transformed into change, lots of it usually, which cascades down through an organisation, and through its many, many projects. Next the change formula as previously described needs to be applied. From this the likely conclusion is: 'Wow this change is really going to disrupt my business and upset a whole bunch of people who really want nothing more than the happy status quo of today (despite most people declaring that 'change is good') and such organisationally driven change will most likely be, at best, passively resisted by the many thereby leading to certain risk and potential failure …'

It is a classic situation – business leaders ask all of their workers three simple questions:

1. What do we want? 'Change' comes the loud reply from all.

2. Who wants change? All hands go up as one.

3. Who wants to change? No hand goes up.

Such a subtle difference there, 'change' versus 'to change' but by creating change within an organisation the leadership team is requiring all impacted 'to change' and that is where it gets personal.

To ensure a successful change it is necessary to use influence and apply strategic thinking in order to create a clear vision as well as identifying those crucial, early steps towards it. In addition, the organisation must recognise and accept the dissatisfaction that exists by communicating industry trends, leadership ideas, best practice and competitive analysis to identify the necessity for change.

At any rate the thought process should go something along those lines with the realisation that change is risky, change is difficult, people will resist change consciously or subconsciously and all of this puts your personal desire for business change at something of a disadvantage compared to not changing (in most cases). By simple extrapolation, you can see that by instigating change you are putting your head on the block, and your job at risk.

And there we have it. Ignore such change dynamics and you will be swiftly pursuing other career opportunities whilst spending more time with your family and overcoming some concerning health issues faster than you can say, 'How did that happen?'.

Yet ignoring these dynamics seems to be the norm in some cases: 'Today's organisation should be agile and flexible as a matter of survival. Companies today face an unprecedented level of change and volatility, ranging from increased M&A activity and regulatory and risk complexity, to new technologies and skill requirements', says PwC in *Human Change Management: Herding Cats*. They go on, 'But the road to agility and change success is often blocked due to people-related issues. Research tells us that as many as 75% of change initiatives fall short of expectations due to employee resistance and lack of clarity and leadership support'

2.4 Making the change for better change

The Gleicher/Beckhard/ Harris formula has one interesting component that is relevant to this book and that is the CL part of the equation; the creative leadership to navigate towards the vision.

Creative leadership can be considered the ability to devise, and implement, innovative solutions, especially in the face of structurally complex or changing situations. It is practised by those people who, when all is shifting and new approaches are yet unknown, can still create clarity of purpose for their teams. These are leaders who seek to navigate and even benefit from the unpredictability that surrounds them.

It is easy to lead when no change is required, although we can all also see that such leadership is not true leadership, and note that no change usually means overall failure at some point in time – sooner or eventually. Stagnation of a business is organisational suicide, it may take months or perhaps years but it will happen.

If you consider the factors outlined:

- D = Dissatisfaction with how things are now
- V = Vision of what is possible
- F = First, concrete steps that can be taken towards the vision
- CL = Creative Leadership to navigate towards the vision

Most (and I say 'most' cautiously), most people impacted by such a change driven from a strategic initiative might acknowledge some dissatisfaction with the status quo (we are back to the 'we want change' here), but only a very few would have a vision for what is possible. The majority will have to be clearly led on those first few steps to the change – all would need that creative leadership for sure – and guess what, the majority will also have a good dose of resistance to the change – that final, balancing R, resistance ('we don't want to change').

To aid your own creative leadership and to offer some practical first steps on how to deliver better overall change within your organisation in Chapter 3 we will delve into five keys to success (with associated challenges). These are:

1. Getting an accurate, transparent, relevant view from the top. You need a clear picture of all the changes that are currently being undertaken in your organisation. This in turn offers an informed platform for considering future, new or alternative changes.

2. Project sponsorship. This is a critical business skill that so many organisations fail to invest in. Project sponsors are the senior owners for projects/changes, the people who represent the investment from the business end and who are ultimately responsible for the success or failure of any changes.

3. Adding change representation at the C-level. Investment in a Project Management Office (PMO) and, potentially, in a Chief Projects Officer will ensure representation of all change to the highest level.

4. Knowing the value of your change. Exactly how much has the business at stake with all of these changes, in terms of both investment and impact. How much of this investment will truly bring about progressive change as opposed to just treading business water or complying with regulatory demands?

5. Professionalisation of project management. The custodians of change delivery need to be the best that they can be, to support the sponsors and the business leaders in making strategic ideas a reality.

These five keys will offer a solid platform for change realisation.

Having explored why it is now time to alter the way that C-level executives drive change, looked at what that change means – to organisations and the individuals which comprise such organisations – we now can begin to identify what might be done within your own organisation to change the way you manage change.

The five keys we have just briefly considered are the focus for the next chapter, each with a challenge related to the key which allows you to assess the 'state of health' of your organisation against each key.

Later on in the book we will cover five further test points to apply against the keys so that you can drill down where you need to in order to assess your own organisation in a truly objective way.

And finally, we will look at five simple steps to move forward with all of the above in a controlled manner, to make sure you, and your peers, do not get fired!

It is the 5-5-5-5 model for successful change delivery.

Progress lies not in enhancing what is, but in advancing toward what will be.

Khalil Gibran

3

How to achieve successful change

It is now time to consider success. How should you change your thinking and what should you do differently in order to avoid getting fired for mismanaging change?

I offer up five challenges to all organisations that are significantly project driven:

- The challenge of investing in the right portfolio dashboard (getting a good and accurate view from the very top)

- The challenge of investing in real professional project sponsorship, executive leadership (project sponsors are from Venus)

- The challenge of investing at the C-level in a chief projects Office and, ideally, a PMO (added to the C-level)

- The challenge of investing in the means to know the true status of your strategic change/project investment (having good analysis and good reporting)

- The challenge of investing in professionalising the project capability and competence within your organisation (professionalise your project management).

We'll visit each in turn.

3.1 Get a view from the top
Challenge 1 – invest in the right portfolio management

Knowing the value of your investment in change, and the consequential cost of failure to deliver this change, is critical.

I want to start by going back to my rallying cry from the Introduction to this book: 'Executives – stop failing your projects!'

The statement was deliberately provocative but I have seen that in all many cases, it is absolutely justified.

The cry from the heady heights of corporate towers is 'Who is responsible for these project failures?' swiftly followed by, 'Bring me the head of a project manager…'. But while the project manager may be the obvious target for blame, it is hardly ever this simple.

The project manager may have failed in some way but who is ultimately responsible for the project's success or failure? Why the sponsor is, of course. I say 'of course' but it astonishes me how many people, people who should know better, people who are senior executives, don't realise – or admit – this to be the case.

The person who is ultimately responsible for the project's success or failure is the sponsor and the sponsor should be at the executive level. We'll cover this in Challenge 2, but back to Challenge 1 for now, investing in the right portfolio dashboard.

We have already considered that the declaration should not be 'Executives – stop your failing projects' but should instead be 'Executives – stop failing your projects'.

So how can you get across the message that executives need to stop failing their projects without looking like a project manager with a chip on their shoulder?

Fear is one way, so why not try this simple exercise when you get the opportunity. Putting a price on something works well, I find.

Start with your company project portfolio value (this should be a reasonable reflection of the strategic investment). For the sake of this example I am going to use pounds sterling but of course it works with any currency. I am also going to use a small portfolio value of say £20m; again please insert your own figure here.

The next step will depend on the type of industry you are in but if we choose a typical regulated commercial model for a business it can be said that out of that total portfolio some projects are compliance driven and some business driven. In this example we will use 40% as compliance and 60% as business growth projects. Therefore, in this example we have £8m invested in compliance projects and £12m in business development projects, again insert the appropriate figures for your organisation. A regulatory light organisation may devote only 20% of portfolio to compliance, with 80% devoted to growth. You know your business so I will leave it up to you to decide.

But we don't stop there. For each project to be sanctioned there must be a 'value added' benefit. For compliance projects this might be expressed better as cost impact. So failure to deliver 'X' will result in a potential fine of 'Y', and/or a potential loss in self-certification of 'Z' and so on. All such failures have cost impacts. This may be a 2:1 ratio calculated as the potential penalties for non-compliance plus the actual project-investment costs. In our example this would be £8m multiplied by 2 plus the original £8m, which equals £24m.

Now for the rest of the portfolio, the business growth or development projects. There would be no point in investing £1 to gain £1, there has to be a return on investment. In terms of a ratio that typically might be at around 4:1 (apply your own business factor here you should be able to find relevant figures in your business case approval process). Therefore, investing £1 would gain a return in investment of £4. Using the same maths as the compliance projects we now have in our example a total of £12m multiplied by 4 plus the original £12m, which equals £60m.

We now have a 'true' project portfolio value of £24m plus £60m which gets us to a chunky £84m.

And guess what? We haven't even considered disruption of business costs during the projects. What shall we say here, maybe another 20% of the total portfolio investment, so about £16m or so?

but the two types of project don't really behave in the same way. I suspect that the 40% we allocated as compliance project investment has a greater success ratio than the other projects. It is not that these projects are any more 'healthy' but the fear of non-compliance ensures that the company throws resources at these projects in a way that it doesn't with the 60% that are business development projects, ensuring 'success' the hard (and costly) way.

Now if the compliance projects are 'successful' (he says smiling knowingly), then the other 60%, the growth projects, must carry even higher levels of potential failure.

Work out these figures now. In our example we will use 10% across the whole portfolio for simplicity.

Can you work them out? Do you have the data (the accurate and real data) to do this? If not, does that worry you? (It should.)

Looking back at our portfolio we said 40% was compliance activity and 60% was business growth but think about it, on balance how many of these growth projects represent real clear blue strategic change? I bet that most are just to keep pace with your market and perhaps only 10% of projects represent real change. So again if failure is the 'norm' and the focus on success tends towards the compliance end of the project scale, how successful is this 10% – the true change projects you have underway in the organisation?

I realise that all of these figures are open to interpretation and maybe my maths is a bit rough but you can see the general idea. It is a little like fantasy finances but the underlying points are that a) your portfolio is bigger than you think it is and b) unless you are in the special minority you probably don't have a really good insight into how this portfolio investment is being managed and how the organisation's money (and future) is being protected.

In our example this takes a £20m base portfolio right the way up to £105.6m.

P	Portfolio value (starting value)	£20m
C/G	Compliance (@ 40%)	£8m (40% x £20m)
	Growth (@60%)	£12m (60% x £20m)
CI	Cost impact – compliance (2:1)	£16m (2 x £8m)
VA	Value add – growth (4:1)	£48m (4 x £12m)
TSF	Total so far	£84m
D	Disruption (@20% of initial portfolio value)	£16.8m (20% x £84m)
F	Failure factor (10% of growth – planned value add)	£4.8m (10% x £48m)
TPV	True portfolio value	£105.6m (TSF+D+F)

Figure 4 True portfolio value

Extensive investment in strategy through projects needs to be backed up by real commitment to successful delivery and, whilst the development of good project managers backed up with appropriate processes and methods is critical, it is the clear responsibility of the executive leaders to connect such strategy to project activity and to sponsor these projects in a competent way.

Hopefully putting a value on the portfolio will have woken up the executives (or even you). Just in case you still don't have their undivided attention why not remind them of this statistic from the introduction to this book:

A four-year study by LeadershipIQ.com, which interviewed more than 1,000 board members from 286 public and private organisations that fired, or otherwise forced out, their chief executive found that the number one reason CEOs got fired was ... wait for it ... mismanaging change!

And what is change if not projects?

Peter Greenwood, group executive director – strategy, CLP Group agrees. In *Why good strategies fail: Lessons for the C-suite* he notes that, 'Companies fail or fall short of their potential not because of bad strategies, but because of a failure to implement good ones'.

Just to be clear that means failure to implement change – which in turn means failure to implement projects – which in turn means failure to be good custodians of the organisation's portfolio.

3.2 Project sponsors are from Venus
Challenge 2 – invest in non-accidental project sponsors

'We are unique individuals with unique experiences' John Gray, *Men Are from Mars, Women Are from Venus*

Men Are from Mars, Women Are from Venus is a book written by relationship counsellor John Gray. It has sold more than 50 million copies (a handful more than my own best-selling book *The Lazy Project Manager*[6]) and spent 121 weeks on the US bestseller list.

The book and its central metaphor have become a part of popular culture and so I found myself, as I thought about my ongoing (since 2011) Campaign for Real Project Sponsors, that maybe we could think of project managers and project sponsors in similar terms.

The book states that most common relationship problems between men and women result from fundamental psychological differences between the sexes. The author exemplifies this through the book's eponymous metaphor: that men and women are from distinct planets – Mars and Venus respectively – and that each sex is in tune with its own planet's society and customs, but those of the other are alien to it.

Now it is possible that this comes into play if, say the project manager is a man and the project sponsor is a woman. (I explored this in the book *Strategies for Project Sponsorship* (Management Concepts Press) with my co-authors Vicki James and Ron Rosenhead, where – at Vicki's suggestion – we agreed to separate the roles by gender.) But for now let's simplify the situation by assuming that gender plays no part in this.

For project success many sources of authority[7] boldly declare that

---

6 In *The Lazy Project Manager* (2nd Edition) Peter Taylor reveals how adopting a more focused approach to life, projects and work can make you twice as productive. *The Lazy Project Manager* has been the project management book to own in the last six years and now this new edition brings the art of lazy productivity bang up to date. Available in all good bookshops ...

7 For starters, check out the Project Management Institute, Inc. Pulse of the Profession™, March 2013, *CHAOS Manifesto: The Year of the Executive Sponsor* (Standish) 2012 and PricewaterhouseCoopers LLC, 'Insights and Trends: Current Portfolio, Programme, and Project Management Practices 2012 - The third global survey on the current state of project management', as just a few.

good project sponsorship is critical but sadly the reality of the situation is less than perfect sponsoring. Often – very often – project sponsors will have received no training or support for their critical role. In Strategies for Project Sponsorship we confirmed that, with 85% of organisations surveyed declaring that they had 'sponsorship in place' but 83% confirming the worrying truth that they did nothing to support, train or guide these project sponsors.

Many speak of the 'accidental project manager' but the reality is that the current generation of project sponsors can also be considered the 'accidental project sponsors'. Although they may not have any background in project management or project-based activity, having reached a senior level within their organisation based on other achievements, they have assumed or have been given that role. Remember that there is not currently any official body of knowledge for project sponsors to help them understand best project sponsorship practices.

And yet project sponsors don't just need to support projects; good project sponsors also support the project manager and project team. It is said that a project is one small step for a project sponsor and a giant leap for the project manager. Wouldn't we all feel so much better if we knew that the project sponsor's one small step would ensure that the complementary giant leap would lead to a safe and secure final landing?

The project sponsor/project manager partnership is one that really needs to be built on a relationship of trust and mutual objectives. As John Gray says, 'If I seek to fulfil my own needs at the expense of my partner, we are sure to experience unhappiness, resentment, and conflict. The secret of forming a successful relationship is for both partners to win.'

Project sponsorship is not about an either/or situation but a win/win, with both the project sponsor and the project manager benefiting. It is, after all, about the project and therefore about the business benefit.

If we look at the flipside of project success, we can see this the consequences of getting this interconnection wrong:

%	Reason	Sponsor	Project manager
40	Unrealistic goals	✗	
38	Poor alignment of project and organizational objectives	✗	
34	Inadequate human resources	✗	
32	Lack of strong leadership	✗	✗
21	Unwillingness of team members to identify issues		✗
19	Ineffective risk management		✗

Figure 5 Typical reasons for project failure

This list of typical project failure issues clearly shows that a lack of good project sponsorship can contribute to unrealistic goals, poor alignment, lack of resources and lack of leadership – in this case the project manager from Mars has one heck of a gaping hole to try and fill due to the lack of professional engagement of a project sponsor from Venus. Equally with a lack of good project management this contributes another vacuum of leadership, team engagement issues and poor risk management – in this case the project sponsor from Venus has no hope of dealing with the consequential impact.

In *Strategies for Project Sponsorship* we found that the best of project sponsors operated in a very balanced way, being involved in the project, being objective about the project, being supportive of the project and project manager, and being reactive to project needs. The project manager clearly needs to be equally balanced.

We also found that the best project managers understood what a good project sponsor should do and how they, as project managers, needed to behave within the reality of the partnership, and with the project sponsor that they were 'given'. As the saying goes, 'you can pick your friends but you can't pick your relatives,' and it has to be appreciated that the same is true of project sponsors.

Each project sponsor (and each project manager) will be different, will be imperfect, and will have strengths and weaknesses but if the two individuals understand each other's responsibilities and capabilities then a balanced, effective and positive relationship can be achieved (and subsequent project success). To once again quote John Gray, 'Relationships thrive when communication reflects a ready acceptance and respect of people's innate differences.'

This needs to be taken seriously and if the relationship is not working changes need to happen, fast.

There is some fantastic work going on with and for project managers. We have landed on Mars and we are setting up home and making it look pretty good (in most cases, Challenge 5 does look at this in more detail); but the weight of effort is all on that side of the scale. Venus, on the other hand is comparatively undeveloped and in need of a real make-over.

In 'Project Management Institute, Inc. Pulse of the Profession™, March 2013' it was assessed that the value impact on poor project sponsorship from the executive level had real significance. The report suggested that with regard to meeting project goals there was a +29% variance with good sponsorship in place but when there wasn't good project sponsorship in place there was a -13% variance of project failure, that is there was a 13% greater chance of the project not delivering what was expected.

Investment in project sponsorship is evidence that the executives are taking strategy investment seriously, whereas not doing so can be seen as an example of the C-suite failing its own business and investors (and projects).

If we think about this in terms of the portfolio we valued earlier (we started with £20m and ended up with £104.8 remember?) doing nothing to develop good project sponsorship would mean that 13% of the value of the portfolio (£13.6m) could practically be written off from day one. Even if you only take the portfolio starting value – £20m – you are losing £2.6m.

How would your CFO feel if you asked him to take £2.6m in banknotes and stuff it in the shredder right now? If anything not investing proper C-level support in strategy is worse than this, since besides the huge financial loss you have to consider time and effort: all those people wondering what they have been working on all this time only to see negative returns.

I hope that the point is now well made – investment in professional project sponsors who see this as an integral part of their role is critical to your organisation protecting and benefiting from your portfolio of investment.

More can be seen in the appendices on this subject. We will consider the executive to sponsor to project relationship in the next chapter under 'ESP'.

3.3 Add to the C-level
Challenge 3 – invest in a chief projects officer

Why a chief projects officer?

Or even why a chief change officer?

Well it starts with strategy formulation which is no longer the annual exercise it used to be – nowadays it is an ongoing iterative activity.

And since each strategy gives birth to one or more projects the portfolio is being updated constantly. Often, it has to be honestly admitted, this happens in some form of infinite capacity model – where the attitude is just keep adding projects and leave the task of sorting out the resources for later (something we will explore more later on).

The idea of a chief projects officer (CPO) is not new but it has begun to emerge recently, with more organisations investing at this level in one person to represent change programmes at the highest level. If you think about CEOs being most often fired for mismanaging change then it really is a 'no-brainer'. If your portfolio is a large one the role of CPO is often more significant than you might think.

When project management, projects and change are elevated to the C-level of importance, one of the distinct advantages is they can no longer be viewed as optional, distracting, annoying, special or unimportant by other business functions. A CPO, or whatever title you may wish to bestow on this position, should make the management of change initiatives across an organisation easier. Equally it should reduce that organisation's exposure to the impact and potential realisation of major risk, and can drive lower costs through economies of scale. All of which should deliver better results across the board, with higher engagement of all stakeholders and impacted employees.

A CPO is typically responsible for providing governance over an organisation's internal projects – external, or customer facing projects can be also covered but that is entering a slightly different world – with a focus on:

- Ensuring all projects support the current strategic objectives;

- Managing the overall portfolio risk to the organisation;

- . Driving efficiencies in delivery and economies of scale;

- Managing resource requirements across the project portfolio;

- Ensuring that all change is led by a skilled professional project management community;

- Leading and being aided by, the PMO;

- Reporting to the executive team.

And how can you get a CPO?

Well, why not fast track one through the project world?

I have seen in the companies that I have worked for, and I am sure that you have all seen it as well, the special ones amongst us that are on a fast track up through the organisation, destined for the hallowed ground of C-level appointment. We all watch in awe, and wonder at their skill, and ability to acquire new skills and master new responsibilities and generally do a whole better than us (unless of course you're already at the C-level in which case 'well done').

And there is nothing wrong with that at all. They experience the company as broadly as possible with time spent in finance, sales, marketing, manufacturing and even sometimes in services. They get first-hand experience of the component parts of the businesses that they will one day lead and this is really valuable preparation. These are the individuals identified as having future leadership potential and any company will invest in such people for their joint futures.

Sadly, I have yet to see a future C-level executive work their way through the project arena, the PMO, the project management practice. One could be forgiven for thinking that the project side of the business (as opposed to the operational side of the business) is perceived to be a little less important, a little less attractive.

There is a danger of course in putting a non-project person in charge of projects.

A comment from my recent PMO Survey summed it up thus:

The management in charge of the PMO are highly experienced operational managers, each with a significant and solid track record. Unfortunately, that expertise does not translate into projects where the deadlines, delivery management and interaction between different role-players are significantly more acute than in operational management.

Perhaps the C-level executive is not immediately destined for the PMO leadership role but surely there is a critical need for such future leaders to understand the nature of their increasingly project-based activities.

May I suggest that a good starting point is for project management executives to talk to the powers that be and the fast track talent development agencies in your organisations, and open up your PMO with an invitation to 'come on in and enjoy the experience'.

In the long run it will only benefit the PMO, your projects, your career and, of course, the organisation. Projects are here to stay and with the increase in project activity inside organisations then really the next generation C-levels should understand as much as they can about our world.

What is a PMO?

Here we should perhaps give a bit more detail on the subject of PMOs, an acronym for Project Management Office, Programme Management Office, or indeed Portfolio Management Office (see appendices for much more information on this).

The PMO in a business or professional enterprise is the department or group that defines and maintains the standards of the business processes, generally related to project management. The PMO strives to standardise and introduce economies of repetition in the execution of projects. The PMO is the source of documentation, guidance and metrics on the practice of project management and execution of project delivery.

A good PMO will base project management principles on accepted, industry standard methodologies, as well as government regulatory requirements as applicable. Organisations around the globe are defining, borrowing and collecting best practices in process and project management and are increasingly assigning the PMO to exert overall influence and evolution of thought to continual organisational improvement.

Establishing a PMO group is not a short-term strategy to lower costs. Recent surveys indicate that the longer organisations have an operating PMO group the better the results achieved in the accomplishment of project goals (which might lead eventually to lowering costs).

Some relevant comments about PMOs include:

- 'Established project management offices result in projects with higher quality and business benefits' PWC: Insights and Trends: Current Portfolio, Programme, and Project Management Practices

- 'Building a Project Management Office (PMO) is a timely competitive tactic,' Gartner Research

- 'With projects in many organisations becoming global, involving multiple business units and locations, the benefits of PMO are more visible,' KPMG report – Business Unusual: Managing projects as usual.

PMOs may take other functions beyond standards and methodology, and participate in strategic project management either as facilitator or actively as owner of the portfolio management process. Tasks may include monitoring and reporting on active projects (following up the project until completion), and reporting progress to top management for strategic decisions on what projects to continue or cancel.

More on PMOs can be found in the appendices.

3.4 Know your value of change
Challenge 4 – Invest in good analysis and good reporting

A great place for your CPO, newly appointed after completing Challenge 3, to start is perhaps in project intelligence.

We will come on to the definition of this term in one moment but to begin we need to clearly differentiate this challenge from Challenge 1 - Invest in the right portfolio dashboard, which was all about knowing what your true portfolio value is. Challenge 4 - invest in good analysis and good reporting is all about correctly understanding the status and the health of that portfolio, and all the projects and programmes that make up that portfolio.

This is project intelligence.

There are probably as many definitions of intelligence as there are experts who study it. But perhaps the simplest way to understand it is as the ability to learn about, learn from, understand, and interact with one's environment.

This general ability consists of a number of specific abilities including:

• Adaptability to a new environment or to changes in the current environment;

• Capacity for knowledge and the ability to acquire it;

• Capacity for reason and abstract thought;

• Ability to comprehend relationships;

• Ability to evaluate and judge;

• Capacity for original and productive thought.

Environment in this definition has a broad meaning that includes a person's immediate surroundings, including the people around him or her. Environment in this case can be something as small as a family, the workplace, or a perhaps a project team.

A project, as any project manager would know, is a temporary endeavor, having a defined beginning and end (usually constrained by date, but sometimes by funding or deliverables), undertaken to meet unique goals and objectives, and usually to bring about beneficial change or added value. The temporary nature of projects stands in contrast to business as usual (or operations), which are repetitive, permanent or semi-permanent functional work to produce products or services.

But what if you combine 'intelligence' with 'projects', what could you achieve? Let's proceed to define the specific intelligence abilities in terms of projects:

- Adaptability to a new environment or to changes in the current environment. Projects are all about delivering change and the ability to oversee such change requires a great degree of adaptability.

- Capacity for knowledge and the ability to acquire it. Projects also require a continuous learning process to understand the change that is being delivered, the lessons that are there to be learned. The combined knowledge of the core and extended project team offer the best platform for project success.

- Capacity for reason and abstract thought. Logical application through the methods of project management will deliver a degree of likely success; the ability to 'think outside the box' and supply beneficial adaptations to process and solutions will deliver the rest.

- Ability to comprehend relationships. Projects are all about people and the relationships that exist between them.

- Ability to evaluate and judge. The very essence of project leadership and decision making.

- Capacity for original and productive thought. Problem resolution and the comparative analysis of options is a constant requirement for good project management.

So in all aspects the project demands an intelligent project manager.

But what else is required to support successful project delivery, not from the individual's perspective but from the organisation as a whole?

Here is where our new term, project intelligence, comes in.

Project intelligence (PI) refers to the skills, processes, technologies, applications, metrics and practices used to support successful project delivery from the organisation as a whole.

Common components of project intelligence include:

- Project management skills, maturity and certification (from project contributor through to senior project (or programme) roles);

- Project sponsorship skills and maturity;

- Project methodologies and practices;

- Project management information systems;

- Project (or programme) management office (PMO) activities and focus (supportive, directive, controlling);

- Executive/management skills, maturity and experience in project delivery;

- Project-based organisational maturity;

- Project support technologies (resource management, skills database, scheduling and time management, cost management, etc.);

- Project dashboard and reporting technologies.

Project intelligence aims to support a project-based organisation's successful project capability.

Whilst we may believe we understand all of these components of PI perhaps we should explore a few of them in some detail.

For example, many organisations have a growing capability in project management skills (this is the next challenge, Challenge 5 – Invest in great project management skills) but many do not specifically train beyond the project management role itself. They don't develop great project sponsors (going back to Challenge 2 – Invest in non-accidental project sponsors) nor do they train people to undertake objective lessons learned activities either.

Executives in general have acquired project knowledge – well let's be honest here, it tends to be project experience, usually the painful sort – but few will come close to understanding the mechanics and skills of being a project leader unless they have been through the 'project delivery' world. This is partly covered by Challenge 3 – invest in a chief projects officer but beyond that, why not consider some form of education – projects for the non-project managers – so that the widest audience can understand why projects are different.

And the deployment of project dashboards is, sadly, often a means to either move swiftly away, back to safe operational issues if the dashboard looks 'green' or raise a lot of unhelpful noise when the dreaded 'red' appears – just when the project needs all the positive help it can get. This is the key to Challenge 4 – invest in good analysis and good reporting.

Project intelligence is all about having the very best environment to nurture and deliver project success through the needed skills, processes, technologies, applications, metrics and practices.

Your organisation deserves the best possible knowledge about your change projects and to obtain that project intelligence is required.

Here is another thought

I saw something for the very first time the other day, and it was one of those, 'why on earth have I never seen this before, it is so obvious … ' moments.

I was reviewing a portfolio dashboard at a software vendor and they, as I have seen many times in the past in many systems, offered me views by project manager, business unit, location, value, phase and so on. But then I asked, and was delighted to see (after a simple sort edit) a view of the portfolio by … yes, you guessed it, by sponsor.

And why not?

Portfolio management should be much more than just a prioritisation of projects and resources exercise. It should be the representation in projects (and programmes) of the competitive strategy that will allow business executives to convert their intentions into reality.

So this is pretty serious stuff then.

All of this is placed in the hands of project managers, and they need to be held to task and held accountable but in the words of the Standish Group, 'The most important person in the project is the executive sponsor. The executive sponsor is ultimately responsible for the success or failure of the project.'

So to me, these days anyway, for the executive team to be able to view their portfolio also by project sponsor and to see which of these 'ultimately responsible' people are performing (and which are not, thereby putting the business strategy at risk) is clearly essential.

When it comes to financial accountability, it seems – at least anecdotally – that projects often go over budget, deliver late, and deliver less than was expected … and there are absolutely no significant consequences at sponsor level. No one appears to be accountable and no one gets removed.

Now, if something goes wrong in the 'real' side of the business – sales down, profits falling, share price dropping – then, more often than not, action is taken and someone will be held accountable. Maybe this is because this is seen as 'real' business and 'real' work and as such has to be taken seriously.

Project sponsorship needs the same strength of focus and importance of status. The success or failure of a project is a direct reflection on the sponsor as the keeper of the organisational vision.

A 'sponsor' view of the project portfolio is an absolute key to this in the future I believe, and fits exactly into Challenge 2 – Invest in non-accidental project sponsors as well as this Challenge 4 – Invest in good analysis and good reporting.

Executives – demand this today!

3.5 Professionalise project management
Challenge 5 – invest in great project management skills, not just project managers

And how can you invest in great project management skills? Perhaps we might begin with the PMO.

Since PMOs lead the project management community – either directly or indirectly, according to your PMO model (see appendices) – then by considering what the best PMOs offer we can gain some insight and see that:

- The best PMOs have consistent, repeatable PM practices across the enterprise. All projects are held to the same standards and requirements for success. They have also eliminated redundant, bureaucratic PM practices that have slowed down projects.

- The best PMOs have the most experienced PMs in place and have a programme underway to recruit the best PMs, develop their existing PMs into the best and to maintain this level of quality and experience.

- The best PMOs sponsor training and facilitate communities of practice to promote PM best practices in their organisations. Such communities of practice provide PMs with a forum to share their knowledge and share experiences.

You can see that is not just a matter of recruiting the best project managers. That helps of course, as does developing the best project managers. Nor is it just having the best sponsors in place (we have covered that in some detail already), although having the best sponsors means that there should be a path for project managers to become sponsors.

It is not just about the provision of a 'lean' framework for all of these sponsors and project managers to work to – and by 'lean' I mean that every part should add value and not create unnecessary waste.

And it is not only about having a great project community – think way wider than just project managers in that community – or about having amazing education, mentoring, coaching or any means to raise skills.

It is about having all of the above and anything else you can constructively think of providing in order to create an environment that provides and celebrates great project management skills.

You have more project leaders than you think

I was a great fan of the original Batman series on television[8], (yes the ones that look really quaint these days), which starred Adam West as Batman and Burt Ward as Robin, the two crime-fighting heroes who defended Gotham City on an almost daily basis from a range of great villains, such as The Penguin and The Joker.

Back in the 1960s when this programme aired I loved the perceived violence (without violence – unlike the modern day big screen versions) that ensued when Batman and his trusty sidekick took on the evil geniuses and his (or her) gang members.

Biff! Bap! Bam! Kerpow! Job done!

I was, of course, always Batman when it came to playtime.

Well, let me give you a new version of that style of language to consider – POP, BAP and PAU! Job done!

---

8 Originally published in *Real Project Management* (Kogan Page 2015) by Peter Taylor. *Real Project Management* takes an in-depth look at the challenges we face in running projects in today's complex and global environment. In this ground-breaking work, leading specialist Peter Taylor examines issues such as the complexity of projects, the virtual nature of projects, executive sponsoring, benefits management and international dilemmas integral to completing a project or programme successfully.

Any business consists of two types of work these days, the temporary project based work – led by a project management community – and the regular operational work – led by business managers.

Regular operational work consists of activities undertaken on a daily repetitive basis to keep the business going, such as accounting, production and sales. Business projects are different. They are temporary tasks that the business initiates to promote or build the company on some way, such as new products, marketing campaigns or new offices.

That said they do have some similarities – both operate under some management control, both have budgets and both should have some sort of plan.

Now both work types contribute to an organisation's success in terms of products, services and marketplace standing but things are changing. It seems more and more of business activity is now project based (one major company recently declared that over 60% of their business was now project led). Back to our Batman words – just what do they mean?

POP: Projects as projects, pure and simple. Well probably not simple. More likely complex and challenging, hence the need for a dedicated project manager.

BAP: Business as projects is definitely on the up as organisations strive to achieve strategic goals and maintain/gain market share, remain profitable/successful and differentiate themselves from competitors.

PAU: Projects as usual, a functional state that some companies have already reached, where the project based activity exceeds the business as usual activity. This may be due to the very nature of the business – if it is innovative or new to the market – or it may be down to a more traditional business entering a significant expansion phase or taking an acquisitional path. In this situation each and every business manager needs to understand and acquire effective project management skills in order to stand a chance of being successful.

Job done: Well not quite. Understanding the situation and actually having the skills in-house to make it likely to succeed are very different.

I believe that more and more people will enter the business world having gained the necessary basic and broad project management skills through schools, colleges, universities and other development routes. But each organisation will have to supplement this capability with education regarding how they manage projects in their business. But the future is looking very promising for the world of projects, projects as usual and business as usual I think.

As Batman said in one of the most recent films 'You know that day that you once told me about, when Gotham would no longer need Batman? It's coming'.[9]

To understand Challenge 5 simply take a look at these three arguments:

Project Management will always be a niche capability

- It's the skill and experience of the individual project manager that makes or breaks a project;

- The need for success means that projects have to be driven by a 'niche capable' project manager;

- General managers will never have the time, the experience, the training, or indeed the skills, to manage any project beyond that which is simple in its goals;

- No executive gets promoted because of their project management skills; they get promoted for other reasons. Executives do

---

9   *The Dark Knight* (2008) Warner Bros., Legendary Entertainment, Syncopy

not need project management skills but project sponsorship and product ownership skills.

Project management is a core skill

- If you believe, as most evidence is now directing us, that we are moving to the projectification of society, where work is less and less a line activity and delivered in the majority through projects, then it is clearly vital that all managers now understand the dynamics of projects and have basic skills and understanding of the process of project management in order to make the most out their organisation's investments;

- All managers need to think in terms of controlled and carefully monitored delivery of outcomes, against a fixed budget and expectations of a quality outcome, that is as projects;

Project management is both a niche capability and a core skill

- Project management methodology is a 'core skill' that all managers need to be aware of but, the actual project management activity is still a 'niche capability', for which additional training and experience are required in order to be successful;

- Managing a small, simple project is no big deal and most people can do it. Managing a large, complex project with substantial risk, diverse stakeholders, a geographically distributed team, multiple constraints and high stakes is best reserved for experts;

- The successful business of the twenty-first century recognises the value of niche project managers working under a supportive executive that has a foundation of project core skills.

I personally believe that there will always be a need for project managers, but what is also needed these days is a new management capability of successful project delivery. One man can't do it all on his own (even Batman has Robin by his side).

All of which, I believe will make you reconsider the full project delivery capability within your own organisation, and then consider how well you and your organisation are supporting all of these project leaders.

In order to completely address Challenge 5 – invest in great project management skills – not just project managers – for as many people as possible to ensure that 'projects' are appropriately understood, and supported as a consequence.

We have now explored the five key challenges

- The challenge of investing in the right portfolio dashboard (getting a good and accurate view from the very top);

- The challenge of investing in real professional project sponsorship or executive leadership (project sponsors are from Venus if you remember);

- The challenge of investing at the C-level in a chief projects officer and, ideally, a PMO (added to the C-level);

- The challenge of investing in the means to know the true status of your strategic change/project investment (having good analysis and good reporting)

- The challenge of investing in professionalising the project capability and competence within your organisation (professionalise your project management).

It is now time to take stock, and to assess your own organisation's position with regard to these five challenges.

We will now cover five test points to apply against these 5 elements before moving on to describe five simple steps to move forward with all of the above in a controlled manner.

When you are out of control,
someone is ready to take over

Toba Beta

4

Are you out of control?

Thinking over what you have read so far, can you answer the following question?

'Do you think that you (your executive team) are in control?'

If the answer is anything but an 'absolutely 100%' then the following are five simple tests to assess how 'out of control' that your organisation is and, how you might begin to get under control with some objective baseline measurements.

4.1 The true value of change

We have already identified that knowing the true value of your investment in change, and the consequential cost of failure to deliver this change is critical.

On that basis now is the time for you to do a bit of maths and work your change portfolio investment out. An example was covered in 'Challenge 1 (on page 40) so you can reference that if you wish.

Before you start the actual calculation, how big do you think your portfolio is right now and how big do you think it really might be? It will be interesting to compare later on.

OK, now take your Portfolio value. The figure doesn't have to be 100% accurate – you are looking for a rough order of magnitude (ROM) really – but if it is really difficult to even gauge a ROM valuation you might consider why that is. How can your organisation manage change if it doesn't know the basics?

Assuming that you do have that number to hand now all you need to know is the ratio of compliance projects to growth projects. If you struggle to identify that percentage mix does this again indicate some fundamental organisational difficulties? But remember, it is just a rough estimate that is needed for this exercise.

Next select or identify the cost/impact ratio and the growth/value add ratio. These really should be part of your business case approval process, by the way.

Finally, you will need estimates of disruption ratio percentage (use the 20% provided if you don't have a true idea of your own organisation's percentage) and failure factor ratio percentage, but only for the growth projects (again, use the 10% provided if you don't have a true idea). For the compliance projects failure is usually something more like some serious fine or restriction on trading. If you can quantify this that's great – it may well be significant – but don't stress too much over this figure.

P	Portfolio value (starting value)	£
C/G	Compliance (@ 40%)	£ (40% x 'P')
	Growth (@60%)	£ (60% x 'P')

CI	Cost impact – compliance (2:1)	£ (2 x 'C')
VA	Value add – growth (4:1)	£ (4 x 'G')
TSF	Total so far	£ ('C'+'G'+'CI'+VA')
D	Disruption (@20% of initial portfolio value)	£ (20% x 'TSF')
F	Failure factor (10% of growth – planned value add)	£ (10% x 'VA')
TP	True portfolio value	£ ('TSF'+'D'+'F')

Take the test

Now run the numbers and then step back and take in the figure at the end.

There you have it – the truth, the whole truth, and most likely, scarily nothing but the truth.

4.2 ABI evaluation

ABI stands for 'allocate, burn or invest' and is a way of looking at how organisations truly manage their change investments after they are sanctioned.

From the previous control test of portfolio value you will now know the 'what', that is, 'What is the value of our change investment?', which is an excellent start.

Now we come to the 'so what' part.

'So, what do we do with this change investment?'

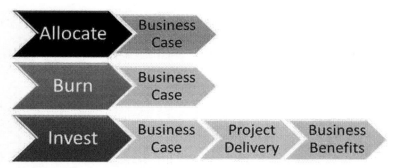

Figure 6 The 'ABI' test

The 'allocate' stage is when an executive team takes the first part of the process very seriously and exhausts many, many hours scrutinising business proposals and change propositions, evaluating alternatives and options, pondering long and hard, challenging and re-challenging the change advocates before allocating the money. At the same time (in much the same way as in the Men in Black films[10]) they erase from their minds the change investment and everything that just occurred in order to carry on with the rest of their business responsibilities and business as usual.

Following the allocate path gives no ongoing control of the changes that have been launched and success is very much dependent on the underlying organisational team and the priorities as it sees them. Success is possible but far from ensured.

The second answer to, 'So, what do we do with this change

---

10 The Men in Black films are science fiction action comedies adapted from The Men in Black comic book series created by Lowell Cunningham and Sandy Carruthers. The films star Tommy Lee Jones and Will Smith as two agents of a secret organisation called the Men in Black who supervise extra-terrestrial lifeforms who live on Earth and hide their existence from ordinary humans.

investment?' is 'burn'. The allocate option works to some degree if there is some maturity of project delivery inside the organisation, it works if there are people who care, in a way that it doesn't work if these are not in place. In this situation the allocate actually becomes a burn.

Anything that is approved will be left to burn away (think of it as money on a bonfire) and be destined to not deliver most or any of the expected business benefits. Without management and control and accountability, alongside that maturity in change delivery, the money will be wasted. Not truly burnt but a little used here and a little there, a resource 'borrowed', and a little help provided over there on that other important activity. The bottom line is it will go and the benefits will not replace its disappearance.

The third, and final, answer is 'I' – 'investment'. Here we are in that happy place where the executive team takes the first part of the process very seriously and exhausts many, many hours scrutinising business proposals and change propositions, evaluating alternatives and options, pondering long and hard, challenging and re-challenging the change advocates and then finally allocate the money. But this time they do not forget all about it. They remember, they care, they engage, they get updates and ask for status analysis and business benefit realisation progress and so much more.

Forgetting 'burn' (and I think you will agree we should) then 'allocate' means to distribute (resources or duties) for a particular purpose, which is a bit of a one-way process, whereas 'invest' means to 'put resources (money) into a commercial venture with the expectation of achieving a profit'. It seems less of a one-way process and more of a 'two-way/we'd like to get something back' process to me.

This requires ongoing and continual interaction with the change in hand.

Take the test

Think of your own organisation and (honestly) decide if you are an 'A', 'B' or 'I' type of executive team. You might even take your analysis down to the individual executive team member (or make it personal to yourself perhaps) asking 'is this person', or 'am I' an 'A', 'B' or 'I' type?

Once you know this you can contemplate what this means for that big number you came up with in 'The true value of change' exercise.

4.3 ESP connection

Another quick test of control is the executive board to sponsor to project manager relationship, or the ESP connection test.

Let's start with the simplest form of this test by asking 'Is there a connection?'.

Does the executive team interact with project sponsors on a regular basis; are they perhaps the executive sponsors themselves? And do the sponsors interact and engage on a regular, reciprocal manner with the project managers?

Come up with a 'No' for either of these connections and you have trouble ahead. You do need all three parties to be connected and communicating.

If you don't declare a complete and utter 'No' then the next step in the ESP test is to consider any weak points in this 'Executive board to Sponsor to Project Manager' or ESP relationship. Here we can return to the question of whether the executives understand change (and projects), and whether the change sponsors understand what it means to be such a sponsor, and how to fulfil that role. Finally, we need to analyse whether the project manager knows what they are doing: do they have experience and are they supported in skills, tools and method?

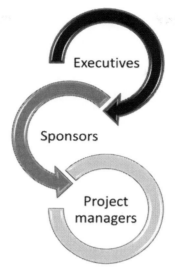

Figure 7 The ESP connection test

Such a consideration will allow another perspective on the robustness of your entire change management structure and to focus where there is a need.

One point here. If there is a problem at say the 'E to S' connection and also at the 'S to P' connection, then the priority has to be to focus and fix the 'E to S' problem first as the higher up the chain of connection the issue is the greater its potential impact, in my personal experience.

Take the test

Consider each level on the ESP connection and evaluate the change leadership maturity at each level – then assess the strength of connection at each of those touch points, 'E to S' and 'S to P'.

Once you have done that focus on the weakest point and put efforts into strengthening that point for the future though awareness, education, shared experience, external advice. In other words, in any way that you can.

4.4 Cycle of engagement

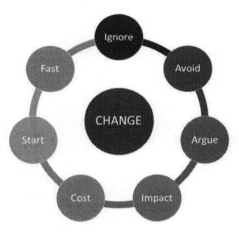

Figure 8 Cycle of engagement

The cycle of engagement (some also refer to this as the cycle of resistance, but that might be considered somewhat cynical) describes some typical stages in a project. Not stages of the project lifecycle you understand but stages of even getting to the project lifecycle, in getting the project started – despite the business case being approved and the project being well and truly 'in the portfolio'

It usually begins when a corporate change initiative is approved and announced, and everyone cheers loudly. A kick-off meeting (party), fueled by marketing spend is completed.

Next, a department or team is asked to pick up the project and implement the change in relation to their day to day work. And that's when the cycle commences ...

Step 1 – Ignore

Take a project logoed beanie hat and mouse mat from the programme kick-off meeting and put them on your desk. Then actively ignore the project for as long as humanly possible, through non-communication.

Step 2 – Avoid

When ignoring the project no longer works you must instead loudly welcome the project initiative and then ensure your department or team dodges involvement through any avoidance tactic you can think of.

Step 3 – Argue

When called out on this behaviour start arguing that you really aren't the best team/department/group to be active at this point in time. If you can get away with pointing the finger at an alternative (and clearly in your opinion, better placed) team/department/group to go before you jump at the chance – it may buy you more time

Step 4 – Impact

Extend your argument to demonstrate that the impact is too much to bear right now and if only you could wait a few weeks/months/ years (delete as appropriate) everything will be so much better and you can really focus.

Step 5 – Cost

A cost argument always gets people's attention, especially if you can challenge the assumptions on the initial business case. If you can point to another team/department/group better placed (i.e. more cost effective aka cheaper) to go before you then go for it.

Step 6 – Start

Despite your best efforts you will in all likelihood eventually reach a point of acceptance (more than likely as a result of you wanting to keep your job) and the project, the change, will finally be undertaken in your department/team/group. Dig out those logoed goodies and shout 'hallelujah' – make sure everyone hears.

Step 7 – Fast

Immediately ask a) what is the fastest way to get this done and dusted and b) can we just copy another team/department/group and make the change – even if it doesn't really fit our needs?

You see what is happening here – no real commitment or buy-in, only lip service to the change and the value of that change.

Back to that classic we saw earlier on isn't it? We all say we want change and loudly cheer the idea – but nobody wants to change.

In order to ensure a successful change, it is necessary to create that clear vision and to make sure people are on board with the change.

Take the test

If you recognise this behaviour inside your organisation then you definitely have an attitude issue and your organisation needs to engage seriously with organisational change management[11] (OCM), and invest time in making people realise that this stuff is important.

4.5 Parachute or catsuit[12]

Challenge 4, if you remember, was all about investing in good analysis and reporting so that the precious portfolio of change is well looked after and cared for, in a kind of management by exception sort of way.

This book is not intended to advise you on what portfolio reporting or dashboard solution to choose and it is not about how you should go about implementing such a solution (I did suggest one specific dashboard view you might ask for from any supplier and/ or solution though so make sure you lock that one down).

But I would like to offer some general advice and it is in the area of scale or being 'fit for purpose'.

In my book *Project Branding: Using Marketing to Win the Hearts and Minds of Stakeholders*, I mention a great presentation by Tom Peters, where he talks about organisations that get so big that they

---

11 Organisational change management (OCM) is a framework structured around the changing needs and capabilities of an organisation. OCM is used to prepare, adopt and implement fundamental and radical organisational changes, including its culture, policies, procedures and physical environment, as well as employee roles, skills and responsibilities.

12 If a catsuit doesn't suit, feel free to replace with wetsuit or any other tight fitting clothing you might prefer.

forget about some of the basic, simple, everyday stuff.[13]

He produces a tiny shampoo bottle that he has taken from a hotel bathroom and he asks, rhetorically, 'who was the average user of this bottle?' The answer being that most likely this was going to be used by a middle-aged business traveller who more than likely wore reading glasses. He then asks, still rhetorically, 'where was this likely to be used?' And the answer this time is of course it would be used when the middle aged business traveller, who most likely wore reading glasses, was taking a shower. He pauses for effect and sums up: this product was most likely to be used by this guy in a shower without his reading glasses on in a steamy environment, with water running, when he wanted to decipher between the two almost identical bottles of shower gel and shampoo. Result: frustration and improper use of products.

A definition of fit for purpose is 'good enough to do the job it was designed to do', but you could argue that the shampoo bottle, standing next to the shower gel bottle, and sometimes also next to a 'body lotion' bottle, is fit for purpose. The trouble is when you want to wash your hair, you need to distinguish the shampoo bottle first to then use it and for it to truly become 'fit for purpose'.

When it comes to reporting this very much applies. Your portfolio reporting process and solution needs to be fit for the purpose to which you wish to put it, practical, usable, understandable, and with the right data in it.

Yes, you can have the all-singing, all-dancing, let's take this barn and put on a show with fireworks and banners approach and good luck to you – you might need a fanfare but almost certainly not. This is the 'parachute' approach, making the solution so copious and all-covering that there is no danger of being exposed in any way. But guess what? Underneath that parachute it is hard to make

---

13 Originally published in *Project Branding: Using Marketing to Win the Hearts and Minds of Stakeholders* (RMC Publications, Inc. 2014) – author Peter Taylor

your way around, and it isn't particularly suitable for most needs (unless you are actually jumping out of a plane of course but this is a metaphor not a freefall). Furthermore, it leads to a lot of wasted material.

The alternative approach is to make your solution as minimal as possible, only the bare data available, lean and focused, tight as can be – this is the catsuit approach. It does the job, precisely and nothing more. It is a good looking solution and may well work, but in all likelihood someone will want something extra (and justify that they need it) and suddenly there's an unsightly bulge and you find yourself expected to make alterations, but without any spare material the bulge is likely to cause an embarrassing rip.

The sensible approach is, of course, somewhere between the parachute approach and the catsuit approach. A bespoke, tailored suit would do very nicely.

Make it fit for purpose, just don't take the whole 'fit for purpose' too far.

Take the test

Look at your reporting and ensure that it is right for your needs, the executive team's needs, and the business needs. Can you access the data you need to make the right decisions? Is that data accurate and timely? Does it truly represent the change underway inside your organisation?

If not then best do something about that fast or you will be making ill-informed decisions, or worse no decisions at all.

4.6 Avoiding the truck wreck

We have talked through the five simple tests of reality and aligned them with to the five challenges, and perhaps, just perhaps, you are feeling pretty good about your organisation. It may not be perfect but you have a rough idea of the value of your portfolio, you generally invest in your change at the highest level, you have an acceptable executive board to sponsor to project manager relationship, and you know what? There is a good appreciation of the value of change among the employees, and they are engaged.

All good then.

Maybe, maybe not. Consider this.

If your organisation typically adopts very rapid strategy changes and is supported by a slow-moving and uncontrolled project management community, then there is a real danger of something like this happening:

Figure 9 Uncontrolled overload

In this photo the cab of the truck is the executive team, planning strategy and steering the company in the direction and speed dictated by the market as they see it. They want to make a difference and succeed. And they will be driving change throughout the business. This means projects.

But think of the trailer as the portfolio of projects underway, undertaken by project managers working hard to deliver success by balancing resources and priorities, while keeping pace with executive demands and responding to their executive sponsor's direction and encouragement.

Now imagine what happens if the executive board tries to slow down suddenly, or change direction without care for the heavy project portfolio load behind them – moving first one way and then the other and then back again.

Do this once too often and the sheer momentum of the project-based activity will just drive it past the strategy control. This is when you end up with a jack-knifed company, projects everywhere and a C-level team helpless to recover the situation. They can only watch as all the other trucks pass them by whilst they wait for the rescue team (assuming there is a rescue team that is – it's more likely that the board will now be considering other options – bringing us all the way back to the 'getting fired' idea).

There is an ongoing danger that organisations need to be aware of: the combination of rapid strategic changes supported by a slow-moving and uncontrolled project portfolio and community threatens organisational stability and may well bring all change to a sudden and very messy stop.

Just like that!

At the start of this chapter we asked one question: 'Do you think that you (your executive team) are in control?'

To help answer that we took five simple tests of reality and aligned them with the five challenges to assess how 'out of control' your organisation is, and how you might begin to bring it under control with some objective baseline measurements.

If the answer to, 'Do you think that you (your executive team) are in control?' was a 'No', we need to go a stage further and progress to the five simple steps to safety before we can move forward with our strategy in a controlled manner.

Of course, if the answer was 'yes' then congratulations, stop reading and pass this book on to someone who needs it more.

They always say time changes things, but you actually have to change them yourself.

Andy Warhol

5

The 5-5-5-5 model

You might possibly be wondering where are we heading with all of this, and now is as good a time as any to introduce you to the 5-5-5-5 model in more detail, if for no other reason than to demonstrate that there is method in all this madness.

This book has followed the path of the 5-5-5-5 model – looking first at the five key elements that provide a successful change foundation inside an organisation, then at the five challenges that you can take on board to make a real difference, after which came the five tests of whether you do need to take any specific action in any of these areas.

And now, finally, we arrive at the five steps that will bring you all the way round to build that successful change foundation if it isn't already in place.

Figure 10 summarises this for easy reference.

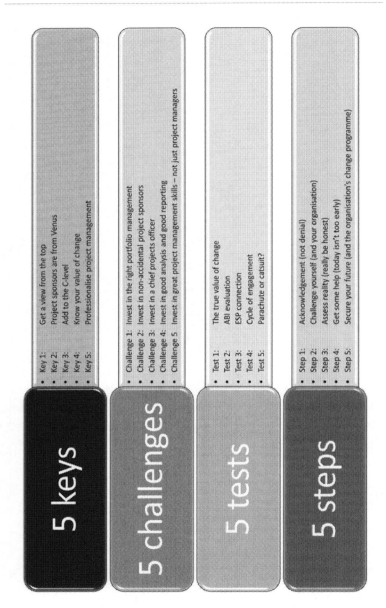

5 keys
- Key 1: Get a view from the top
- Key 2: Project sponsors are from Venus
- Key 3: Add to the C-level
- Key 4: Know your value of change
- Key 5: Professionalise project management

5 challenges
- Challenge 1: Invest in the right portfolio management
- Challenge 2: Invest in non-accidental project sponsors
- Challenge 3: Invest in a chief projects officer
- Challenge 4: Invest in good analysis and good reporting
- Challenge 5: Invest in great project management skills – not just project managers

5 tests
- Test 1: The true value of change
- Test 2: ABI evaluation
- Test 3: ESP connection
- Test 4: Cycle of engagement
- Test 5: Parachute or catsuit?

5 steps
- Step 1: Acknowledgement (not denial)
- Step 2: Challenge yourself (and your organisation)
- Step 3: Assess reality (really be honest)
- Step 4: Get some help (today isn't too early)
- Step 5: Secure your future (and the organisation's change programme)

Figure 10 The 5-5-5-5 model

And there you have the backbone of the five keys, five challenges and five simple tests of reality aligned to these challenges so that you can assess how out of control your organisation is, and how you might begin to bring it under control with some objective baseline measurements.

Now we can progress to the five simple steps to safety in order to move forward with all of the above key elements in a controlled manner.

6

How to take back control

The five key challenges have been laid out, you have completed the five simple tests of reality (and know the truth about your organisation) and so we can progress to the five simple steps to safety in order to guide your organisation to a better place – change wise that is.

This is the last step on the 5-5-5-5 model's path to not being fired at the C-level.

6.1 Be the person who puts the 'C' for change in the C-level

If there is a problem something must be done – somebody has to do something about it.

Since you are reading this book it might be safe to assume that the 'someone' is going to be you. Hopefully not on your own of course.

If you do find yourself alone in this situation, why not get some help? If it is about bringing a reality check to your executive team, then help is at hand – just check out the appendices for ideas around presentations and workshops on offer that can bring this reality to your organisation and executive team.

Getting help is one of the five practical steps you can take, as we will see.

6.2 Five practical steps

6.2.1 Step 1: Acknowledgement (not denial)

In self-help the first step to recovery (from anything from bereavement to compulsive gambling) is acknowledgement that there is a problem. So that is where we will start.

Acknowledgement is the acceptance of the truth or existence of something and/or the recognition of the importance of something.

Denial is a statement that something is not true, perhaps the refusal to acknowledge an unacceptable truth or emotion or to admit it into consciousness, and is often used as a defence mechanism.

Step 1 is to take the problem to a point of acknowledgement instead of leaving it in a soggy pit of denial. You might do this by:

- Reading this book (you have, so an excellent start).

- Sharing this book with your peers/executives (or better still buying multiple copies).

- Researching external guidance or insight. Who is your accountancy firm/systems integrator and what do they have to say on the matter of change and projects?

- Talking to other similar organisations if you have an opportunity – in industry communities, or at conferences, etc.

- Running an open meeting or workshop to uncover any issues or concerns the executive may have.

- Analysing poor performance with regard to change and asking the question, 'Why?'

6.2.2 Step 2: Challenge yourself (and your organisation)

Once you reach a state of 'acknowledgement' then the challenge and the question of what needs to be done can be presented to the executive team. Just how bad is the problem, and who cares enough to try and make a difference?

This is the ideal way to move on to the challenges facing your organisation but you may have to merge steps 1 and 2 if only partial acknowledgement of there being a problem is achieved.

The five challenges in this book are used as the basis for this step. You don't have to use all of them, just the ones that make for interesting reading and that highlight the problem (or problems).

- Some potential problems might include:

- Investing in the right portfolio dashboard.

- Investing in professional project sponsorship and executive leadership.

- Investing at the C-level in a chief projects office and, ideally, a PMO.

- Investing in the means to know the true status of your strategic change/project investment.

- Investing in professionalising the project capability and competence within your organisation.

6.2.3 Step 3: Assess reality (really be honest)

The GROW[14] model is a simple method for both goal setting and problem solving.

If your organisation reaches a happy state of 'acknowledgement' of the problem and has reviewed the 'challenge' (or challenges) then it is now time to set a goal in place to make change better.

One of the foundations for such goals to be achieved is to also achieve an honest (no matter how tough and unappetising that may be), clear and no-stone-unturned reality check.

This is the second stage of the GROW model (see table opposite).

Step 3 is to make understanding of the facts a reality within your executive team.

Ideas for achieving this include:

- Brainstorming the situation with your executive team.

- Opening up the situation to input from a wider employee base. Those at the coalface often know a lot more than you might think, and care a lot more as well.

- Considering history, what has prevented you from realising and/or altering the way you oversee 'change'?

- Taking insight from external references, such as books, articles, papers, etc.

- Considering what the future would ideally be like, the goal in the GROW model, and working back from that future state to the now to highlight obstacles.

---

14 The GROW model, developed in the United Kingdom, was used extensively in corporate coaching in the late 1980s and 1990s. While no one preson can be clearly identified as the originator, Graham Alexander, Alan Fine and Sir John Whitmore all made significant contributions. Max Landsberg also describes GROW in his book *The Tao of Coaching*.

G	The goal is the end point, where your organisation wants to be.	The goal has to be defined precisely, so that it is very clear when it has been achieved.
R	The current reality is where your organisation is now.	What are the issues, and challenges, and how far are they away from their goal?
	There will be obstacles stopping your organisation getting from where it is now to where it wants to be.	What are the known obstacles?
O	Once obstacles have been identified, your organisation needs to find ways of dealing with them if it is to progress.	What options do you have to overcome each obstacle?
W	The options then need to be converted into action steps which will take your organisation to your goal.	These are the way forward.

6.2.4 Step 4: Get some help (today isn't too early)

We briefly mentioned this at the start of this chapter. If you do find yourself alone in this situation, then why not get some help? Even if you are not alone you may still need some help to reach a point of general agreement and in developing a forward plan to move from the 'as is' state to the much preferred 'to be' state of good change leadership.

If your particular issue is bringing a reality check to your executive team, then help is at hand – just check out the appendices for ideas around presentations and workshops on offer that can bring this reality to your organisation and executive team.

Step 4 involves conceding that you need help, and getting it. Places you might turn to include:

- The author of this book (https://uk.linkedin.com/in/peterbtaylor) is a real possibility, I am keen to help any organisation deliver change more effectively and more efficiently

- Any experienced organisational change agent.

- Your accountancy firm/systems integrator (if you have lots of money to spend of course ... no only kidding, they do have a real depth of skill in this area and could be the right choice for your organisation, I should know, I used to work for one of them).

- Other organisations that may have been through a similar process.

6.2.5 Step 5: Secure your future (and the organisation's change programme)

Once enlightenment is achieved, reality accepted and a plan put in place to bring about a new understanding of change inside your organisation then your job, and that of the executive, is to lead.

The best way to do this is to remember a key truth: children learn by example, and so does your team.

Step 5 is therefore leading by example. You and your peers need to embrace the new ways of leading and managing change, and show true enthusiasm for this new order. Model the way you want your team to behave by:

- Embracing the new ways;

- Showing and sharing enthusiasm;

- Being creative in the ways you encourage others to change;

- Being open to feedback and comment, with the aim of becoming even more successful in the future.

6.2.6 The Starbucks moment

Not a step as such but rather my recommendation based on many years of experience.

In life it is important to celebrate everything that should be celebrated and enjoy those special moments as well.

So what is the 'Starbucks moment'?

Well firstly it has to be noted in the interest of objectivity that other coffee vendors are available, I am not specifically recommending Starbucks, but I experienced a 'moment' in a Starbucks and since then have thought of it as the Starbucks moment. Please feel free to call it what you wish.

The details of my own 'moment' aren't really important but suffice to say, it was a moment of clarity and huge emotion and it was, without doubt, one of the special moments in my life.

(The coffee was OK as well, tall caramel macchiato if you're interested, and I even had a cheese and marmite sandwich to go with it. But this is all incidental.)

My point is that we all have moments such as these, some small and some big (some perhaps even life-impacting) and it should go without saying that, in these moments – or very soon afterwards – you should recognise what has happened and celebrate.

In bringing about change, big change, significant change, strategic change, it is often difficult to remember what it is all for – when you are neck deep in alligators you can lose sight of the fact that you are there to drain the swamp. But throughout the change lifecycle there are moments that need celebrating – with your executive team, your project sponsors, your project managers, their teams, and so on.

Take the time to identify and recognise these moments, take a breather from the whole 'alligator' issue and focus on all you have achieved so far and celebrate it. It doesn't have to be a big party with all the works (nice when that does happen of course), but it can be small – a pat on the back, a smile and a thank you, a gift (a Starbucks gift card perhaps), in fact anything at all that recognises the 'moment'.

On the subject of alligators, I was very recently on an airboat in the Florida swamps spotting alligators – wonderful fun.

The captain of the airboat, Cap'n Fred as he was known, told us how to avoid being eaten by alligators. The common myth is that you run in zigzags as alligators can only run in straight lines but Cap'n Fred said this was rubbish. According to Fred, the best way to avoid being eaten by an alligator was to 'trip up the guy next to you and then keep running'. Cue appreciative laughter. But this doesn't hold true in our world.

In the change world it is all about no-one being left behind. You need each and every person, and one way to ensure everybody survives the project is to spot those 'moments' and celebrate them appropriately.

Make sure you know when you, or someone near you, has had a Starbucks moment and enjoy that moment in style – it will really, really help deliver all of that change.

6.3 A start, not an end

And there you have it – you are only at the very start of a journey, a journey that may well be a difficult one, but a journey that is most definitely worth taking.

I hope that this book and its contents have helped you a little on your way.

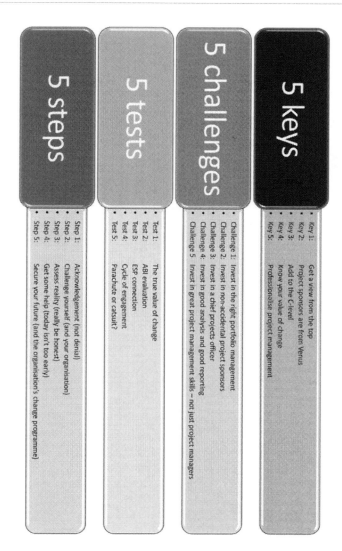

5 steps

- Step 1: Acknowledgement (not denial)
- Step 2: Challenge yourself (and your organisation)
- Step 3: Assess reality (really be honest)
- Step 4: Get some help (today isn't too early)
- Step 5: Secure your future (and the organisation's change programme)

5 tests

- Test 1: The true value of change
- Test 2: ABI evaluation
- Test 3: ESP connection
- Test 4: Cycle of engagement
- Test 5: Parachute or catsuit?

5 challenges

- Challenge 1: Invest in the right portfolio management
- Challenge 2: Invest in non-accidental project sponsors
- Challenge 3: Invest in a chief projects officer
- Challenge 4: Invest in good analysis and good reporting
- Challenge 5: Invest in great project management skills – not just project managers

5 keys

- Key 1: Get a view from the top
- Key 2: Project sponsors are from Venus
- Key 3: Add to the C-level
- Key 4: Know your value of change
- Key 5: Professionalise project management

Figure 11 The '5-5-5-5' Model

At this point you may utter the words 'And how much will all this investment cost?'

But that is the wrong question. The right question is on the opposite side of the business equation: 'What will it cost if I don't invest?'

Go back to the 'true value of my portfolio' exercise results (page 67) and you will see exactly why this, and not, 'How much will it cost to invest?' is the right question.

What is that I hear you say? 'What will it cost if I don't invest?'

Good question – well done.

Incredible change happens in your life when you decide to take control of what you do have power over instead of craving control over what you don't

Steve Maraboli, motivational speaker and behavioural scientist

7

A final thought

At the very start of this book I included a dedication. Perhaps you skipped it in your eagerness to get to the nitty-gritty of making a success of your business strategy, so I'll reiterate it:

> *'I would like to dedicate this book to the real custodians of change – from the executive leaders who truly understand change (and therefore projects), to the project sponsors who take ownership and direct that change – and to the thousands of professional project managers who deliver amazing results every day that bring about positive change'*

I truly meant that and genuinely hope that this small book and the ideas within it will help add you to the ranks of real custodians of change around the world.

We need you, your organisations need you, change needs you – and your projects need you.

Thank you
Peter Taylor, March 2017

8

Appendices

8.1 Survey

As part of the research for this book a survey was undertaken, and this was followed by a series of interviews with respondents focused on executive change leadership.

This research identified a pattern of failure, notably through lack of understanding of the project world by C-level executives, and through an associated strategic and organisational change-management failure which came about as a result of both ignorance of and a passivity of control regarding these critical investments.

The survey was conducted during May and June 2016 and received responses from organisations covering the US (35%), Canada (5%), UK (20%), Europe – excluding the UK and Eastern Europe (10%), Eastern Europe (7.5%), Asia Pacific (20%), and the rest of the world (2.5%).

The company sizes were as follows: under 100 employees (12.5%), between 100 and 500 employees (15%), 500 to 1000 employees

(7.5%), between 1,000 and 5,000 employees (20%), 5,000 to 10,000 employees (10%) and over 10,000 employees (35%).

Considering the activity of change these organisations reported that the number of projects that they undertook on an annual basis was: less than 10 (10%), between 10 and 50 (25%), between 50 and 100 (20%) and over 100 projects per year (45%).

Comments on this project activity included:

- The organisation has several levels of project i.e. strategic, divisional, departmental, etc. Only fifteen are directly visible at the C-level.

- The majority of projects are BAU (business as usual) and hence are relatively short and non-complex.

- We currently have a portfolio of thirty-three programmes specifically focused on technology.

- Most projects are relatively small and of low technical complexity but involve significant organisational change.

- Each business unit manages its own project portfolio; if the threshold budget is met then the project gets registered in the global portfolio.

The study gave us valuable insight into the levels of investment businesses make in change as shown in Figure 12, opposite.

Now if we take the mid-point in each of these ranges, with the exception of the 'greater than $100 million' category, where we conservatively just take the figure to be £$100 million, within this data collection we end up with an average portfolio investment of $40,000,000.

One positive result was that more than 10% of responses came from those acting at the C-level or in a board level management role. Not surprisingly the majority (82%) were from the project world: PMO leaders, portfolio managers, programme and project managers.

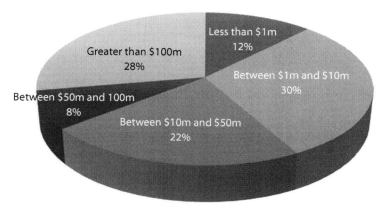

Figure 12 Value of change portfolio

Having secured an understanding of the business background, the next survey question focused around executive sponsorship for change. Here there was a wide range of views with 35% declaring that project-based change had strong executive sponsorship but 22.5% claiming exactly the opposite, that is weak or no executive sponsorship. Another 42.5% suggested that their organisation had a mix of strong and weak executive sponsorship. Form this evidence we might conclude that fewer than 1 in 4 organisations have the necessary strong sponsorship for their change initiatives, which has to be of real concern.

Specific comments here included:

- Project sponsorship is overly complex with multiple responsibilities;

- C-level executives are committed to budget, time [and] quality only;

- Executive group is generally in favour and supportive, however on occasions, usually when under the pump, they try to bypass the processes;

- Recently the company is becoming aware of the importance [of strong executive sponsorship] but we still have a long road ahead to really embrace the benefits of this position;

- It took a watershed event at the turn of the century but has been improving ever since;

- Projects always have an appointed sponsor, but few are either capable in the role or engaged.

And intriguingly one person noted:

- [There are] usually too many sponsors.

The next question was, 'Thinking about the C-level (or highest role in your organisation) do you feel that they understand project management?' only 17.5% felt that they could honestly answer 'yes' to this, while 20% felt that the answer to the question was a very clear 'no'. The remaining 62.5% suggested once again a mix, some do and some don't being the thought.

This was all qualified with various comments, including:

- It's hard to say they 'completely' understand, but I think they have a >80% understanding.

- Torn between this rating and 'not at all', some do get it, but that does not mean it is effectively applied.

- We are fortunate enough to have two very dedicated developers who have been in the business for a long time. Without them we would be up the proverbial creek without a paddle. In the absence of any project management structure whatsoever they struggle through and keep things moving in the right direction. We have fallen into 'scrummerfall' management with the team jumping from one random task to another. Flexibility for flexibility's sake, we rarely achieve anything from one week to the next and time-boxing is the stuff of mythology, or so you would believe working here. As a student of project management with qualifications in PRINCE2 and PMP, and a thesis on agile management, I have never been so frustrated in my working career as I am watching this going on around me!

- Not everyone understands it, some projects fail due to this reason.

- Most do not 'get' project management as they are mostly from an operational career path and not a project one.

- I think it is assumed that C-levels understand what it means to be involved in a project.

- It seems there is a fear factor in taking time to educate and reiterate what project management means and seldom do people ask.

There were some further concerning notes when it came to the next question which was 'And thinking about the same C-level, do they invest the right amount of time in overseeing the change that your projects deliver to the business?' Responses included:

- Some sanction the business case then move on.

- If it is their pet project, then they do anything to get it through otherwise they tend to sit in the background and wait for the project manager to approach them.

- Some projects suffer from lack of support once they are in execution.

- C-level executives often pay attention to them when projects are in trouble.

- Depends on the size, scope and you'd get range of answers from project management practitioners to portfolio leads (i.e. C-level view of total change portfolio).

- If the topic is the flavour of the month then yes, otherwise no.

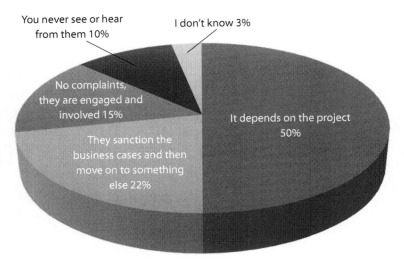

Figure 13 C-level investment of time

The 15% who get engaged and involved must be praised, but the rest?

The 10% who are never seen or heard from clearly are putting other matters ahead of change, while the 22% who sanction the business case and move on seem not to care about business benefits achieved, as opposed to conceptual pre-change business benefits calculated. As for the 50% in the large 'depends' category, well who really knows, but it doesn't sound too good.

All in all, this seems a weak foundation for investments averaging $40 million, as previously calculated.

Considering this, the final question explored instances when a C-level manager had been removed, replaced or resigned because they mismanaged a significant change (project) and the results here were interesting to say the least.

Nearly a quarter (22.5%) of respondents stated that one, or in some cases more than one C-level manager, had indeed been removed, replaced or resigned because they had somehow mismanaged a significant change (project). One contributor dryly noted that whilst there may well have been such failure 'Sponsorship can change for myriad reasons but I have never seen any public acknowledgement of mismanagement' and a second one said, with feeling, and perceptible despair, 'Executives come and go. We, at the project level, know if they are good or not at leading change but the company doesn't want to hear the truth or indeed offer a means of sharing such truth. We just get on with at the project level and try to fill the gap.'

Finally, before we move on to some of the case studies that resulted from the survey, here are a few final thoughts from our respondents:

- He who shouts loudest gets his projects approved. The KPIs are solely based on the success of their division, and not the group, therefore they care little for the portfolio being designed and managed correctly and delivering strategy.

- The fact that we have taken two years from development of strategy to establishment of the project portfolio tells its own story.

- As PMO manager for two years I have developed the project management capability across the organisation and there is now a sense among some of the executives that the job is done. I need to show value in management of the portfolio or I fear that they will shut down the PMO and use the money elsewhere.

- Generally speaking, the biggest issue is the assumption that C-level executives know how to sponsor a project because they are C-level executives, when more often than not they really appreciate (gentle!) guidance on how to actually be a sponsor.

- Project management here is treated as an administration role with emphasis placed on ensuring no complaints or escalations are rendered by the sponsors, which results in too frequently doing the wrong thing at the wrong time, [so] a few months after implementation [the project] gets abandoned and processes revert to their pre-project state.

One final comment was very concerning, from a change-orientated perspective: 'The CEO of my organisation does not believe in project management'.

Worrying indeed.

8.2 What is the C-level?

I have used, throughout this book (including the very title *How to get fired at the C-level*) the term C-level, and, whilst most readers will understand this common business term, it is perhaps worthwhile taking a little time to cover it in some more details.

C-level is an adjective used to describe high-ranking executive titles within an organisation. C, in this context, stands for 'Chief'.

Officers who hold C-level positions are typically considered the most powerful and influential members of an organisation. Consequently, they make higher-stake decisions, their workload is more demanding, and they have relatively high salaries and associated bonuses, share options and other perks.

Examples of C-level titles include the following:

- CCO (chief compliance officer)
- CEO (chief executive officer)
- CIO (chief information officer)
- CTO (chief technology officer)
- CFO (chief financial officer)

- CKO (chief knowledge officer)

- CSO or CISO (chief security officer or chief information security officer)

- CDO (chief data officer)

- CVO (chief visionary officer)

- CDO (chief data officer, chief digital officer)

- CPIO (chief process and innovation officer)

- CMO (chief marketing officer)

A managing director would be included in this list as an effective C-level executive.

There is current growth in the concept of the CPO or Chief Project Officer, which is a very exciting development from this author's point of view.

8.3 The meaning and purpose of project sponsorship

The following is an extract from the book *Strategies for Project Sponsorship* published by Management Concepts Press (2013) which offers guidance at three levels – for the project manager on how to work with project sponsors, for the project sponsors on how to be an effective project sponsor, and finally for organisations on how and why they need to invest in project sponsorship as a critical business skill.

All over the world, there has been much focus on the training and development of project managers. The growth in qualifications in this area has been immense and is matched by the growth in capability for the majority of project managers. But the lack of maturity of the project sponsor role and the lack of understanding of its importance leave a gap in project management. Our intent is to correct this gap.

Project sponsorship can be many things to many people. Sponsors, especially, may see their role differently from the way project managers perceive it. Sponsorship includes many senses of the word sponsor without a common understanding of the roles and responsibilities to sponsor across project industries.

Professionals may be unclear on a definition of the term, but project management practice gives us some idea of what a sponsor does, as distinct from a project manager, and why it is so important to the success of a project and to an organisation's goals.

What is project sponsorship?

The Oxford English Dictionary offers many definitions for the word sponsor. Used as a noun, it can mean any of the following:

- A person or organisation that pays for or contributes to the costs involved in staging a sporting or artistic event in return for advertising: e.g. 'The production cost $80,000, most coming from local sponsors'.

- A person who pledges to donate a certain amount of money to another person after he or she has participated in a fundraising event organised on behalf of a charity.

- A person who introduces and supports a proposal for legislation: e.g. 'A leading sponsor of the bill'.

- A person taking official responsibility for the actions of another: e.g. 'They act as sponsors and contacts for new immigrants'.

- A person presenting a candidate for confirmation or baptism: e.g.

'Lisa has asked me to be her sponsor for confirmation next month'.

The word can also be used as a verb, meaning:

- To provide funds for (a project or activity or the person carrying it out): e.g. 'Joe is being sponsored by a government training programme'.

- To pay some or all of the costs involved in staging a (sporting or artistic) event in return for advertising: e.g. 'The event is sponsored by Qantas Airlines'.

- To pledge to donate money on behalf of a participant in a fundraising event: e.g. 'Nigella wishes to thank all those people who sponsored her'.

- To introduce and support a proposal in a legislative assembly: e.g. 'The senator sponsored the bill'.

- To propose and organise negotiations or talks between other people or groups: in the U.S., sponsored negotiations between the two sides.

Interestingly, even though the word sponsor has many meanings, there is no dictionary definition that in any way relates to project management and the topic of this book, project sponsorship. So given the lack of an authoritative definition of a project sponsor, and with not a lot written about the role of project sponsorship, let's take a look at how one of the major project management professional certification bodies defines it. According to the Project Management Institute's (PMI) A Guide to the Project Management Body of Knowledge (PMBOK® Guide)[15]:

15 *A Guide to the Project Management Body of Knowledge (PMBOK® Guide)*, 5th edn (Newtown Square, PA: Project Management Institute, 2013), 32.

A sponsor is the person or group who provides resources and support for the project and is accountable for enabling success. The sponsor may be external or internal to the project manager's organisation. From initial conception through project closure, the sponsor promotes the project. This includes serving as spokesperson to higher levels of management to gather support throughout the organization, and promoting the benefits the project brings. The sponsor leads the project through the initiating processes until formally authorized, and plays a significant role in the development of the initial scope and charter. For issues that are beyond control of the project manager, the sponsor serves as an escalation path. The sponsor may also be involved in other important issues such as authorizing changes in scope, phase-end reviews, and go/no-go decisions when risks are particularly high. The sponsor also ensures a smooth transfer of the project's deliverables into the business of the requesting organisation after project closure.

Considering this definition and applying our own observations from experience, discussions, and surveys, we can surmise that a project sponsor is the person in an organisation who will:

- Realise the most benefit to business value from the project;

- Actively seek or provide funding to support the project;

- Set the parameters and expectations for project success;

- Provide high-level monitoring of the project to ensure the expected value will be realised;

- Promote the project to ensure visibility and increase the chance for success;

- Actively be involved in risk identification, management, and mitigation;

- Authorise significant project changes to extend or compress scope, schedule, budget, or quality.

In short, this high-level list shows that the project sponsor is the person in the organisation who most cares about the project and its success. At least they should be.

Every project begins with an idea. The business case, based on that idea, explains the project and its expected benefits. The sponsor must believe in the project and in the anticipated benefits. They will bring the project to the portfolio committee or other authority within the organisation responsible for providing funding. This committee provides funding to the sponsor, with the condition that the sponsor will provide the executive-level project oversight. Now the project can begin. The first steps include selecting a project manager and developing a project charter or other initiating document.

The sponsor's role

Project sponsorship is an active senior management role. A sponsor is responsible for identifying the business need, problem, or opportunity. Once this has been done, the sponsor ensures the project remains a viable proposition and that the expected business benefits are realised. During project performance, the sponsor focuses on resolving any issues outside the control of the project manager and acting as the project's champion.

The role of sponsor is a far-reaching one. It can't be considered a full-time role – unlike the role of the project manager for a significant project – but it does require a depth of knowledge, experience in project activity, a power base of some influence, and an alert and decisive mind.

A project sponsor is not a sponsor for life – that is, she has other roles and responsibilities that don't pertain to the project – but she is there for the duration of the project, from initiation to closure. Randy

Englund and Alfonso Bucero write in their book *Project Sponsorship*[16]:

> *A good sponsor performs different functions during the project life cycle, serving as mentor, catalyst, motivator, barrier buster, and boundary manager. The sponsor is the link between the project manager and senior managers. The project sponsor is the best 'project seller.' The sponsor promotes and defends the project in front of all other stakeholders. Being a project sponsor is to be involved from project initiation to project end.*

Just consider for a moment the complex skill set that the sponsor's duties demand of one individual. It is no wonder that you probably will not get the 'perfect' sponsor for your project, because individuals who can deliver everything that is expected of a sponsor are few and very far between. Furthermore, even people who have the right personal qualities may not be educated in or have experience with the best practices and intricacies of project work.

Sponsors don't just support projects; good project sponsors also support the project manager and project team. It is said that a project is one small step for a project sponsor and a giant leap for the project manager. Wouldn't we all feel so much better if we knew that the project sponsor's one small step would ensure that the complementary giant leap would lead to a safe and secure final landing?

In our experience, the skill profile of project managers continues to grow, which is a good thing, and more and more organisations are developing project managers in a disciplined and mature manner. We hope this means that accidental project managers – those who came to the role by chance and often totally unprepared – are becoming extinct. But it is also our experience that the same cannot be said of project sponsors. Far too many organisations wrongly believe that a

---

16 Randall L. Englund and Alfonso Bucero, *Project Sponsorship: Achieving Management Commitment for Project Success* (San Francisco: Jossey-Bass, 2006), xii.

project sponsor is just a figurehead who is never called to active duty, and so very few ever invest in any developmental support for their sponsors. Being a 'good' project sponsor, like being a 'good' project manager, requires structured experience, education, and guidance; but most of the time, sponsors are left with only what they have learned through hap and circumstance throughout their careers.

This is clearly the wrong approach, and we are certain that it threatens the success of projects. According to a KPMG New Zealand project management survey released in 2010[17] one of the main reasons for project failure was weak sponsorship:

The project sponsor has a critical role to monitor and control the project at [the] strategic-level, steering a project back on track if it runs into difficulties along the way.

One of the fundamental reasons why projects fail is the lack of executive sponsorship and management buy-in. Sixty-eight percent of companies do not always have an effective sponsor to provide clear direction for the project or to escalate problems when necessary.

If 'trying to manage a project without project management is like trying to play a football game without a game plan,'[18] then 'trying to deliver a project without project sponsorship is like playing football without a rule book, a coach, any funds for new players, or even a referee.'[19]

To be a successful partner on a project, a sponsor needs to be

---

17 The full report can be accessed at https://home.kpmg.com/nz/en/home/insights.html

18 Karen Tate, PMP, a past board member of PMI. Collected on the Project Auditors LLC website: http://www.projectauditors.com/Company/Project_Management_Quotes.html.

19 Penned by Peter Taylor for publication in this volume.

connected to the project manager and to the project team. It is a real red flag if she is remote. If she is too busy to meet, to discuss the project, and to help, the red flag turns an even darker shade. If she avoids helping assign project roles and responsibilities, or never has time to approve documents, make decisions, or just be there to advise, there is a problem – one that is reaching critical status. Throw in a dash of blaming anyone but herself for any problems, and it is probably time for you to walk away from the project if you possibly can. The project manager, the project team, and the business are in real trouble – and so is the project.

Bad sponsors will exhibit some or perhaps, in the worst-case scenario, all of the preceding behaviours. Conversely, a good project sponsor does just the opposite. She will happily act as advisor to the project manager and will focus on removing obstacles in the path to project success.

A bad project sponsor may simply be an untrained or inexperienced sponsor, but even if her poor performance is less her fault than the organisation's for failing to invest in its sponsors, she still may be a project manager's worst nightmare.

8.4 The meaning and purpose of a PMO

The following is an extract from the book *Leading Successful PMOs* (published by Gower in 2011).

This book, together with the companion book *Delivering Successful PMOs* (also published by Gower, in 2015) offers a guide to all organisations on how to set up, how to lead, how to design and how to implement a PMO.

Let me start in the spirit of that classic US game show *Jeopardy!*[20]:

Answer: A PMO.

Question: (and therefore actually the correct answer; that is just the way it works on the game show, trust me) What is the department or group that defines and maintains the standards of process, generally related to project management, within an organisation?

Applause from the audience and smiles all round.

Yes, the Project Management Office (PMO) in a business or professional enterprise is typically the department or group that defines and maintains the standards of process, that are generally related to project management, within the organisation.

But I am afraid it is not that simple.

The abbreviation PMO can stand for Programme Management Office (confusingly also a PMO) or Portfolio Management Office (increasingly confusingly also a PMO). There is even talk of a Project Office (PO), a Project Control Office (PCO), a Central Project Office (CPO), and a Project Support Office (PSO). Up to you to choose – what do you have in your company? What are you leading? What are you part of? What is it that you are currently planning?

You may well have a completely different flavour of PMO from the above.

---

20 *Jeopardy!* is an American quiz show featuring trivia in history, literature, the arts, pop culture, science, sports, geography, wordplay, and more. The show has a unique answer-and-question format in which contestants are presented with clues in the form of answers, and must phrase their responses in question form.

The PMO strives to standardise and introduce economies of repetition in the execution of projects and is the source of documentation, guidance and metrics on the practice of project management and project execution.

It is also the body that links business strategy to the projects that such strategies require.

Organisations around the globe are defining, borrowing and collecting best practices in process and project management and are increasingly assigning the PMO to exert overall influence and evolution of thought to continual organisational improvement. Many PMOs will base project management principles on accepted industry standard methodologies such as the PMBOK[21] or PRINCE2[22].

There are as many variances in the structure, format and focus of PMOs as there are definitions of the term.

PMO Types

Typically there are four basic types of PMO:

---

21 *The Project Management Body of Knowledge (PMBOK Guide)* is a project management guide, and an internationally recognized standard that provides the fundamentals of project management as they apply to a wide range of projects, including construction, software, engineering, automotive, etc. The purpose of the PMBOK is to provide and promote a common vocabulary within the project management profession for discussing, writing, and applying project management concepts. The PMBOK is developed by PMI® The Project Management Institute (PMI) is a non-profit professional organization for the project management profession with the purpose of advancing project management

22 PRojects IN Controlled Environments (PRINCE) is a project management method. It covers the management, control and organisation of a project. PRINCE2 refers to the second major version of this method and is a registered trademark of the Office of Government Commerce (OGC), an independent office of HM Treasury of the United Kingdom.

- A departmental PMO

- A special–purpose PMO

- An outreaching PMO

- An external PMO

And then there is a fifth type, an enterprise PMO.

It should also be noted that the enterprise structure can apply in more than one of the first four categories.

Type definition aside, a PMO is a group or department within a business, agency or enterprise that 'owns' the kind of project based activity that cuts across the operational activity. The primary goal of a PMO is to achieve benefits from standardising and following project management policies, processes, and methods. Over time, a PMO will become the source for guidance, documentation, and metrics related to the practices involved in managing and implementing projects within that organisation.

Why invest?
Why do businesses invest in a PMO?

On the one hand, companies of all kinds face the continued fallout from the most recent global recession which has placed an added burden on projects and project managers delivering expected benefits.

On the other, we are part of a dynamic, resourceful and ever-evolving commercial world that demands change as part of its survival; change demands projects, and projects demand project managers.

History is littered with significant project failures (witness some of the statistics of the CHAOS[23] report analysis of IT project success, and more often failure[24]), yet there are also spectacular project success stories linked to the maturing practice of project management.

Those projects that will be commissioned in the future, as well as the ones that are allowed to continue in the current challenging climate, will be expected to deliver greater business benefits, endure closer scrutiny from senior management and are likely to face far more pressures to deliver. There is no longer any room for project failure; projects that are approved need to succeed.

And who will be under the most pressure? You guessed it, the managers responsible for those projects.

Right now our projects, and our project managers, need the help, support and guidance of a good PMO and a good PMO has to be led by a good PMO leader.

The good news is that PMOs are in demand.

---

23 The Standish Group regularly produces the CHAOS reports which research the reasons for IT project failure in the United States, the last report showed that software projects now have a 32% success rate, or put another way a 68% chance of failure. As an example of failure the Standish Group found that the average cost overrun was 43 percent; 71 percent of projects were over budget, exceeded time estimates, and had estimated too narrow a scope; and total waste was estimated at $55 billion per year in the US alone.

24 The Standish Group report has been challenged in the past. With the problem being that it measures success by only looking at whether the projects were completed on time, on budget and with the required features and functions. It does not address such other measures of the quality, the risk, and customer satisfaction. Nevertheless, we can all speak to a project success score of less than 100%.

In their *The State of the PMO*[25] report PM Solutions stated that, 'The upward trend is unmistakable, both in sheer numbers of PMOs and in the rising organisational clout. In our 2000 research on "The Value of Project Management", only 47% of companies had a project office. In 2006, our research on "Project Management: The State of the Industry" showed that 77% of companies had PMOs; now research shows that 84% of companies have PMOs.'

This is excellent news; it suggests the battle to establish the value of the PMO has, for the most part, been won.

This book is therefore less about the business justification of a PMO and more about being the very best that you can be as a leader and a contributor to a successful PMO; making your PMO the one that really delivers.

Projects, programmes and PMOs

To avoid confusion, it is important that we all have a common understanding of project and PMO terminology.

To that end we should align our language when it comes to projects and programmes[26], portfolios and PMOs.

It can be a very confusing world when we talk of projects and programmes and portfolios and project management offices so I am going to open with the simplest of explanations which I am

25 PM Solutions Research. (2010) *The State of the PMO 2010.* Research report. Glen Mills, PA: PM Solutions www.pmsolutions.com

26 The basic difference is between different languages: American English always uses program but British English uses programme unless referring to computers. Australian English recommends program for official usage, but programme is still in common use. The spelling 'program' was predominant in the UK until the nineteenth century, when the spelling 'programme' became more common — largely as a result of influence from French, which has the same word 'programme'.

hoping you will accept for the purposes of this discussion.

I call this 'the PMO declaration'

Figure 14 Portfolio, projects, programmes and the PMO

Project management is all about doing something (a project) in the right way and the 'right way' is all about method, discipline, quality and control.

Programme management is all about doing those things (the projects) in the right sequence or order.

Portfolio management is about doing the right things.

Which leaves the PMO, which I think of as doing all the above but with the right team (the right things, in the right way, in the right order).

Hopefully that helps?

If you prefer a more detailed explanation, then read on.

Project management

Project management is the discipline of planning, organising, securing and managing resources to bring about the successful completion of specific project goals and objectives. It is sometimes confused with programme management,* however, technically, that is actually a higher level construction: a group of related and interdependent projects.

A project is a temporary endeavour, having a defined beginning and end (usually constrained by date, but sometimes by funding or deliverables), undertaken to meet unique goals and objectives, usually to bring about beneficial change or added value. The temporary nature of projects stands in contrast to business (or operations) as usual, which are repetitive, permanent or semi-permanent functional work to produce products or services. In practice, the management of these two systems is often found to be quite different, and as such requires the development of distinct technical skills and the adoption of separate management.

The primary challenge of project management is to achieve all of the project goals and objectives while honouring the preconceived project constraints, or at least in managing the adjustments of these constraints through a disciplined process. Typical constraints are scope, time and budget, together with an over-arching consideration of quality.

Programme management

Programme management is the process of managing several related projects, often with the intention of improving an organisation's performance. A programme of projects can help a company achieve one or more of its strategies. The individual projects within it have varying end dates but the programme ends when the strategy has been reached.

There are two different views of how programmes differ from projects.

In one view, projects deliver outputs, discrete parcels or 'chunks' of change; programmes create outcomes. Thus, a project might deliver a new factory, hospital or IT system. By combining these projects with other deliverables and changes, the associated programme might deliver increased income from a new product, shorter waiting lists at the hospital or reduced operating costs due to improved technology.

The alternative view is that a programme is nothing more than either a large project or a set of projects. In this second view, the point of a programme is to exploit economies of scale and to reduce coordination costs and risks. The project manager's job is to ensure that their project succeeds. The programme manager, on the other hand, may not care about individual projects, but is concerned with the aggregate result or end-state. For example, in a financial institution a programme may include one project that is designed to take advantage of a rising market, and another to protect against the downside of a falling market. These apparently opposing projects fit together in the same programme.

Portfolio management

Project portfolio management (sometimes referred to as PPM) is a management process designed to help an organisation register and view information about all of its projects. Once it has the visibility (you can't manage what you don't measure) then this allows such organisations to sort and prioritise each project according to certain criteria, such as:

- strategic value,

- cost,

- impact on resources,

- tactical need.

A PPM driven organisation will have, typically, a portfolio/project dashboard representing the overall health and status of each project.

It should be noted that the projects and/or programmes within a given portfolio may not necessarily be interdependent or directly related to each other. For example, in a services supplying company the portfolio will mainly record customer project activity with little relationship between the individual projects.

PMOs

The project management office (PMO) in a business or professional enterprise is the department or group that defines and maintains the standards of the business processes, generally related to project management. The PMO strives to standardise and introduce economies of repetition in the execution of projects. The PMO is the source of documentation, guidance and metrics on the practice of project management and execution.

A good PMO will base project management principles on accepted, industry standard methodologies, as well as government regulatory requirements, as applicable. Organisations around the globe are defining, borrowing and collecting best practices in process and project management and are increasingly assigning the PMO to exert overall influence and evolution of thought to continual organisational improvement.

Establishing a PMO group is not a short term strategy to lower costs. Recent surveys indicate that the longer organisations have an operating PMO group the better the results achieved to accomplish project goals (which might lead to eventually lowering costs).

PMOs may take other functions beyond standards and methodology, and participate in strategic project management either as facilitator or actively as owner of the portfolio management process. Tasks may include monitoring and reporting on active projects (following up a project until completion), and reporting progress to top management for strategic decisions on what projects to continue or cancel.

So there you have it. Personally I prefer my simple model – so let's stick to that shall we?

8.5 Workshops based on this book

How to get Fired at the C-level goes beyond the constraints of a book.

To that end the author would like to offer some focused workshops, keynote presentations and insightful supporting education to help organisations achieve the success in strategic change that they desire, and to help C-level executives understand the challenge and benefit from the opportunity.

We have said that someone has to do something – assuming that there is something to do, that is there is or there are problems, of course.

And we also agreed that, if you are that someone, you do not have to do this on your own.

If it is about bringing a reality check to your executive team, then help can be found right here, with the author of this book.

If your organisation or team needs a short sharp executive 'scare' session (or reality check) then Peter Taylor can deliver this, customised for your organisation, your executive team and the time available.

If you need to take it to the next level of detail, you might be interested to learn that Peter Taylor offers two specific workshops based on this book.

Both can be customised to suit your audience's needs and indeed, a fully customised engagement can be proposed if you feel your organisation requires something very specific in order to help you look at what you should be considering and doing to make sure your change, your projects, your organisation and you are still around for the foreseeable future.

Workshop 1: Executives – stop failing your projects!

Yes! You read that right – not 'Executives – stop your failing projects' but 'Executives – stop failing your projects'.

The report *Why good strategies fail: Lessons for the C-suite*, published by The Economist Intelligence Unit Limited in 2013 stated in its conclusion that there was a need for increased C-suite attention to implementation (and therefore projects). It said, 'Leadership support is the most important factor in successful strategy execution, yet a substantial number of survey respondents indicate that the C-suite is insufficiently involved'.

This is why I make the loud and bold challenge that executives are failing their projects and why I strongly believe the situation needs to stop – now!

The workshop will explore the true value of your strategic change portfolio (projects) – which will probably be bigger than you think – and will explain why it, you and your organisation are at real risk of failure (and wasting a lot of that financial investment).

What you should do about this critical situation is, of course, explained simply. The two key actions you need to take to avoid strategic change failure will be introduced, making this undertaking far less onerous than it would have been had you attempted it solo.

Workshop time   1 to 3 hours[27]

Participants   C-level executives and senior project leaders

Workshop 2: Two key actions you need to take to avoid strategic change failure

If you are concerned about strategic change failure, and by association your portfolio of projects, then there are two key actions that can dramatically de-risk this potential situation.

Step 1: Strategies for project sponsorship

It is stated in the Standish Chaos Report, amongst many others, including PMI's 'Pulse of the Profession', that the sponsor is the person who is ultimately responsible for the success (or failure) of the project, who represents the business and the business change. And yet, there is a chasm in many organisations between this statement and the reality of the professionalism and associated investment in development of those active sponsors.

We will explore the current challenges of project sponsorship maturity and offer some techniques for creating an effective sponsorship community as one of the two foundations of project success.

---

27 Workshop timing can be customised to the availability of the audience – the shorter workshop focuses only on the high level issues with minimal interaction time permitted, the longer workshop allows for a 'deeper dive' and with audience interaction and discussion

Step 2: Building the best PMO

Here will explore the true value of a good PMO in guiding project success and supporting the sponsor community in the management of the portfolio of project change.

We explore what is meant by a balanced PMO, a design developed by Peter, as well as presenting a new working model for project management excellence with the project academy concept.

This all adds up to a critical second foundation for project success.

The workshop will be an interactive experience with first-hand case study insights and the opportunity to spend some time with one of the world's most experienced PMO leaders.

Workshop time 2 to 3 hours[28]

Participants   C-level executives, senior project leaders, sponsors and PMO leaders

The workshops are standalone but related and follow the journey from strategy investment through to the key foundations of change/project success.

Also available are keynote presentations on this book, on project sponsorship and PMO leadership – as well as a series of additional inspirational workshops.

---

28 Again here the workshop timing can be customised to the availability of the audience – with the longer workshop allowing for some audience interaction and discussion

8.6 Peter Taylor

Here is a little more about the author of this book, Peter Taylor. You can also find rather a lot about Peter on LinkedIn (feel free to connect), Twitter (feel free to follow), and via your favourite search engine:

- LinkedIn: https://uk.linkedin.com/in/peterbtaylor
- Twitter: @thelazypm
- Web: www.thelazyprojectmanager.com
- Podcast: 'The Lazy Project Manager' in iTunes
- Blog: https://thelazyprojectmanager.wordpress.com/

Figure 15 Peter Taylor aka The Lazy Project Manager

Peter Taylor is a PMO expert currently leading a Global PMO of 200 project managers acting as custodians for nearly 5,000 projects around the world, for Kronos Inc., a billion-dollar software organisation delivering workforce management solutions.

Peter is also the author of the number 1 bestselling project management book *The Lazy Project Manager*, along with many other books on project leadership, PMO development, project marketing, project challenges and executive sponsorship.

In the last four years he has delivered more than 200 lectures around the world in over 25 countries and has been described as 'perhaps the most entertaining and inspiring speaker in the project management world today'.

His mission is to teach as many people as possible that it is achievable to 'work smarter and not harder' and to still gain success in the battle of the work/life balance.

8.7 Other books by Peter Taylor

Peter Taylor is a prolific author with 18 books published in the last seven years.

He authored the number 1 Amazon bestseller *The Lazy Project Manager*, one of the most successful project management books of all time, and he just keeps on writing about things that he is passionate about – such as you not getting fired!

The Lazy Project Manager (2nd edn)[29] (Infinite Ideas)

Strategies for Project Sponsorship (Management Concepts Press)

The Lazy Winner (infinite Ideas)

Leading Successful PMOs (Gower)

The Lazy Project Manager and the Project from Hell (TLPM Publishing)

The Project Manager Who Smiled (TLPM Publishing)

---

29 Translated into German, Italian and Portuguese

The 36 Stratagems (Infinite Ideas)

The Dance of the Meerkats (Infinite Ideas)

The Art of Laziness (Infinite Ideas)

The History of Laziness (TLPM Publishing)

The Lazy Blogger (TLPM Publishing)

The Extra Lazy Project Manager (TLPM Publishing)

Real Project Management (Kogan Page)

Delivering Successful PMOs (Gower)

Project Branding (RMC Publishing)

Get Fit with The Lazy Project Manager (TLPM Publishing)

The Social Project Manager (Gower)

How to Get Fired at the C-level (TLPM Publishing)

8.8 Tailwind PS

 Peter Taylor is delighted to work in partnership with Alex Marson and the Tailwind PS team – very fine purveyors of everything you might need to manage your change successfully.

Tailwind Project Solutions (http://tailwindps.com) was formed in 2014 to provide a bespoke approach to project leadership development. Owned by director and CEO Alex Marson, the organisation works with large FTSE 250 clients including some of the biggest companies in the world in the asset management, professional services, software, automotive, finance and pharmaceutical industries. The company employs a team of world-class experts, who provide a bespoke approach to the challenges faced by its clients. It was formed as a result of a gap in the market for expertise which truly gets to the heart of the issues clients are facing – providing a robust, expert solution to change the way that companies run their projects.

At the time, the market was becoming flooded with training companies, providing a 'sheep dip' approach to project management, and the consensus was that this didn't solve the real challenges that businesses and individuals are experiencing in this increasingly complex world of project management. The vision was to hand-pick and work with the very best consultants, trainers and coaches worldwide so that Tailwind could really make a difference to its clients, to sit down with them, understand their pain points, find out what makes them tick, and learn what is driving their need for support.

These challenges being raised time and time again sit in the project leadership space, from communication issues, not understanding stakeholder requirements or having the confidence to 'push back', lack of sponsorship support, working across different cultures, languages, levels of capability and complexity. We expect more from our project managers – we expect them to inspire, lead teams and be confident.

Tailwind's experience is vast, and includes providing interim resources in the project and programme management space, supporting the recruitment process, experiential workshops, coaching – from project managers through to executives – providing keynote speakers, implementing PPM Academies, undertaking PM Healthchecks and Leadership development. The approach is created – often uniquely – to solve the real challenges of each of Tailwind's individual clients.

It is change, continuing change, inevitable change that is the dominant factor in society today. No sensible decision can be made any longer without taking into account not only the world as it is, but the world as it will be.

Isaac Asimov

29123180R00077

Printed in Great Britain
by Amazon